12 R/S

Designing with wood and metal

Designing with wood and metal

R. Speed and J. N. Ashworth

PHOTOGRAPHY Ian H. Rewcastle
DRAWINGS J. V. Clibbon

Longman

LONGMAN GROUP LTD   London and Harlow
Associated companies, branches and
representatives throughout the world

© Longman Group Limited

First published 1971

ISBN 0 582 32543 9

Printed in Great Britain by
William Clowes and Sons Ltd.
London, Beccles and Colchester

ACKNOWLEDGEMENTS

The authors are extremely grateful to their colleague W. K. Davies, Esq., for his assistance when compiling the notes and checking the drawings, and to past and present students for permission to use photographs of their work.

Contents

Designed and made by

INTRODUCTION   The authors feel that the primary considerations in any design
assignment are those of functional efficiency and aesthetic
relationships, and that, in the main, the materials chosen and the
techniques employed should provide the relief from stark simplicity.
Thus, in this book, the materials used are those considered most
appropriate and so the designers are freed from the limitations of
any one medium.

The first few pages indicate the approach made to each problem
and further illustrations are accompanied by notes and suggestions.
It is hoped that these will stimulate the reader to examine them for
possible qualification to suit his own particular needs.

Designing a coffee table

AREA OF THE TOP   The area of the top should be related to:
(a) The number of people likely to use the table.
(b) The space available in the room.
It can be discovered by setting out the required saucers, plates,
etc. on a table or piece of board.
A compromise may be necessary when the result is checked against
the available space.

SHAPE OF THE TOP   Rectangular, circular, square, oval, triangular. Which is the most
suitable shape? Does it fit in with the existing furniture?

HEIGHT OF THE TOP   The height must allow for comfortable use from easy chairs.

MATERIALS   Top—Wood? Faced chipboard? Plywood with tiles?
                    Blockboard with plastic laminated top surface?
                  Underframe—Wood? Tubular steel?
              Weight must be carefully considered if the table is to be moved
              around the room.

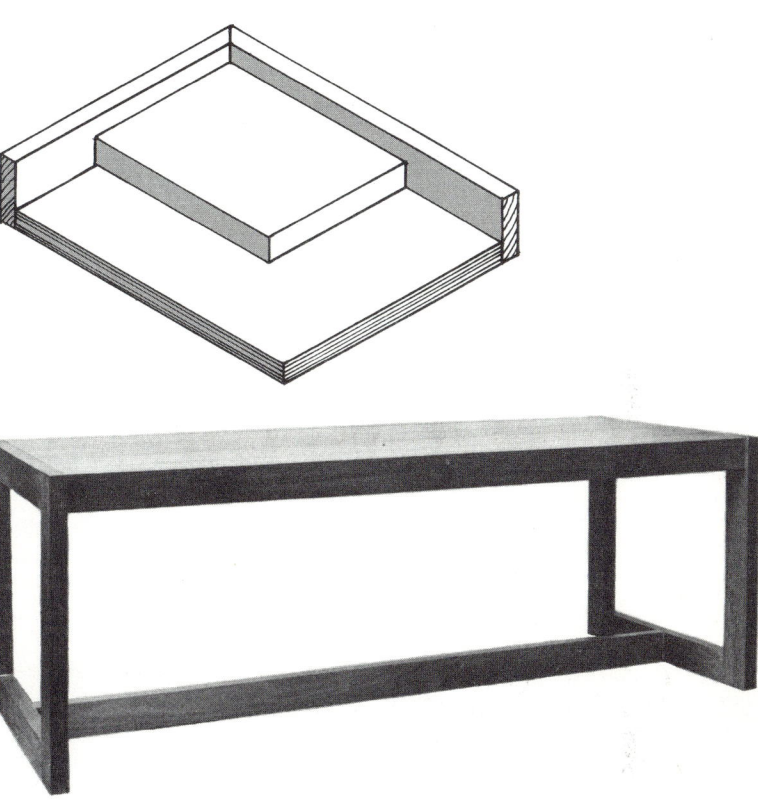

CONSTRUCTION   Having chosen the materials ideas for the construction can be
                 sketched out. At this stage it can be decided whether a magazine
                 rack can be usefully incorporated and what form it might take.
                 Wood slats, split cane, plywood, cord, dowel rod, glass, steel or
                 brass rod?

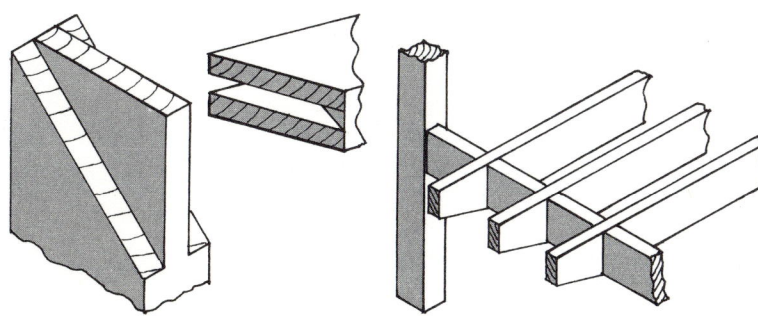

A view in orthographic projection may appear to have pleasing proportions, and an interesting combination of rectangular shapes. But when translated into three dimensions the perspective is altered. Proportion, shape, and line are affected.

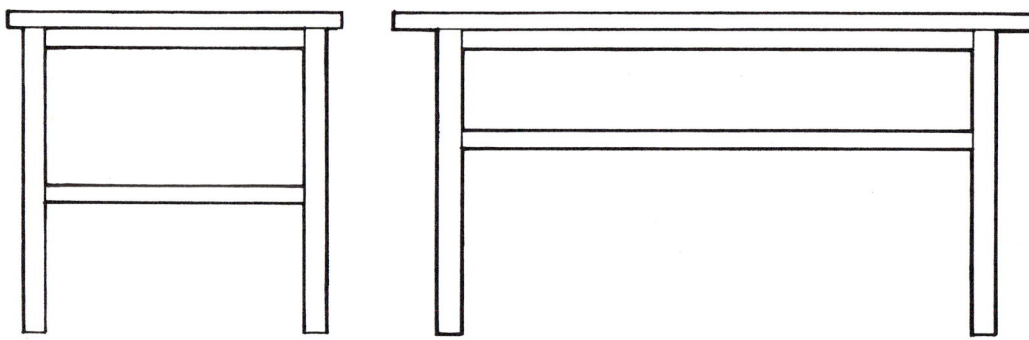

These effects can best be seen by making a full size model. It can be simply nailed or screwed together from scrap strips and hardboard. If the model is 'lived with' for a few days it will soon become apparent whether the table will be suitable for its use and environment. Adjustments can be made easily before making the final working drawing.

FINISH   Without some form of protective surface, wood becomes stained
and dirty. Some timbers can be scrubbed clean, as is the sycamore
of the butcher's table. But in the home a permanent finish is more
desirable. The polish chosen for each job should be suitable for the
material and the use. For example, a coffee table top needs to have
a stain- and heat-resistant surface, but is the same finish necessary
on a bookcase? A carving looks best with the dull sheen of wax, but
if this is applied to a fruit bowl it soon becomes spoiled by the
dampness of the fruit. It is worthwhile trying out the various
polishes to find out which is the most suitable for the wood and the
job, before using it on a completed piece.

Beeswax
Carnauba wax
Cellulose based polish
Shellac based polish
Linseed oil
Teak oil
Polyurethane
Varnish and lacquer
Plastic lacquer with a catalyst hardener

Coffee table

This table is light in weight yet strong and stable.
If the magazine rack is required it can be made of split cane or
thin cord, or have wooden slats.

METHODS OF JOINING SLATS INTO THE FRAME

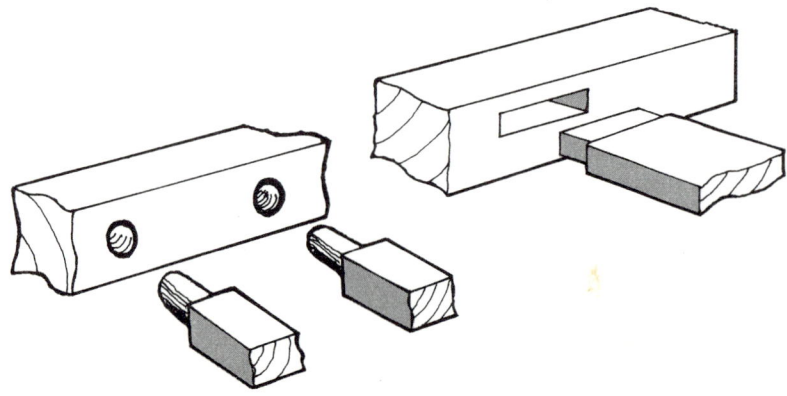

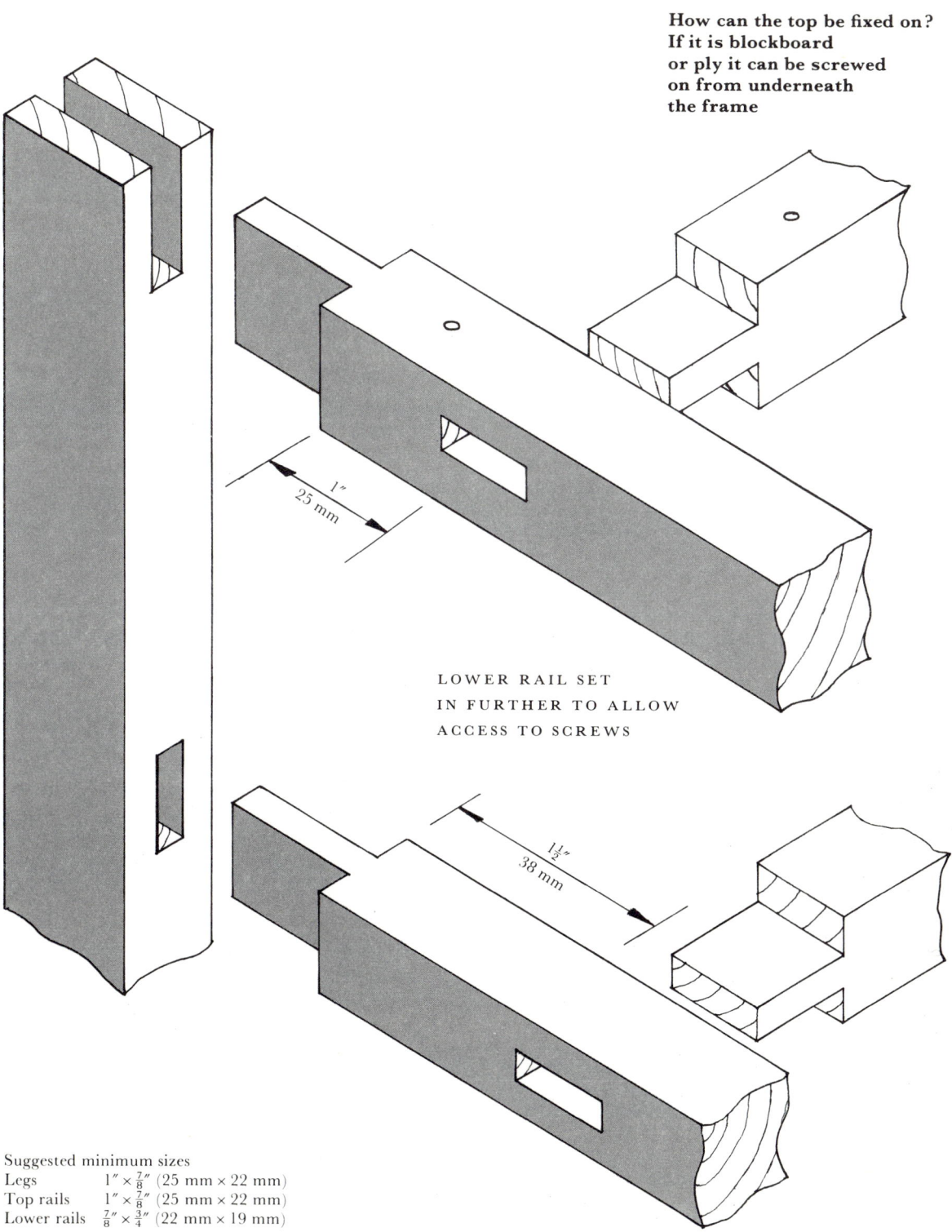

**How can the top be fixed on?
If it is blockboard
or ply it can be screwed
on from underneath
the frame**

1″
25 mm

LOWER RAIL SET
IN FURTHER TO ALLOW
ACCESS TO SCREWS

1½″
38 mm

Suggested minimum sizes
Legs $1'' \times \frac{7}{8}''$ (25 mm × 22 mm)
Top rails $1'' \times \frac{7}{8}''$ (25 mm × 22 mm)
Lower rails $\frac{7}{8}'' \times \frac{3}{4}''$ (22 mm × 19 mm)

Coffee table

The making of a full-size wooden model, lightly nailed together, allowed a variety of arrangements and proportions to be thoroughly considered and discussed before any practical work commenced. This table illustrates how, with careful handling of materials, most pleasing effects can result from a very simple form.

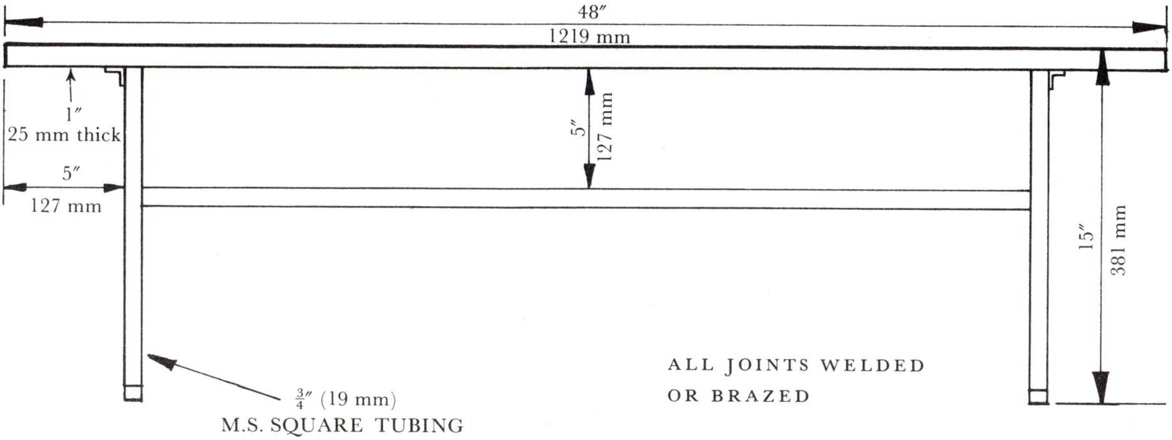

48"
1219 mm

1"
25 mm thick

5"
127 mm

5"
127 mm

15"
381 mm

$\frac{3}{4}$" (19 mm)
M.S. SQUARE TUBING

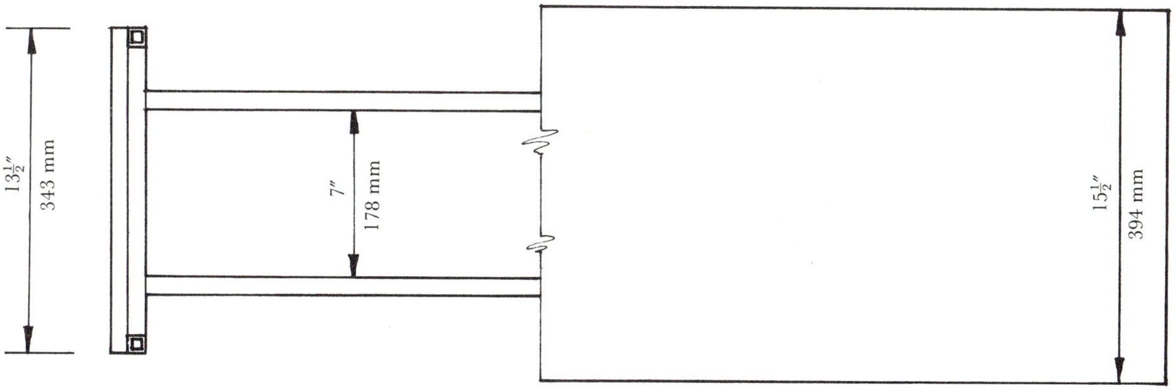

ALL JOINTS WELDED
OR BRAZED

13$\frac{1}{2}$"
343 mm

7"
178 mm

15$\frac{1}{2}$"
394 mm

SCREW SLOT—NECESSARY WHEN
TOP IS OF SOLID TIMBER

**Alternative fixing—
blockboard top**

$\frac{3}{4}$" × $\frac{1}{8}$" angle
(19 mm × 3 mm)

WOODEN FEET—HELD
IN TUBING WITH
'ARALDITE'

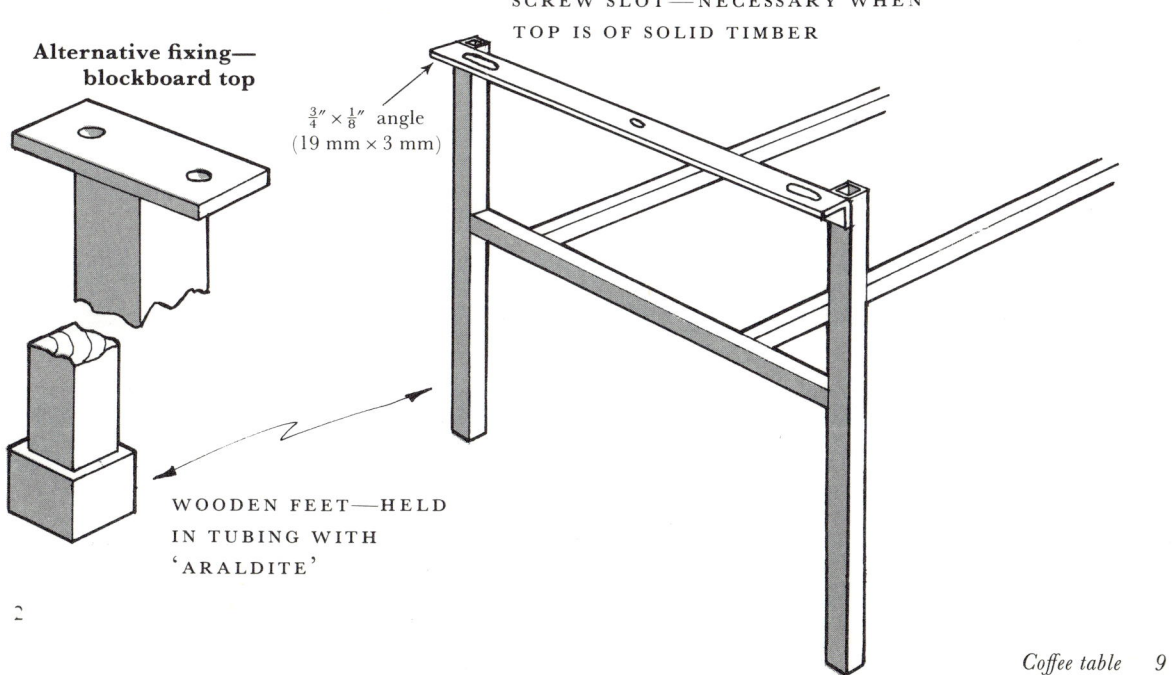

Table seat

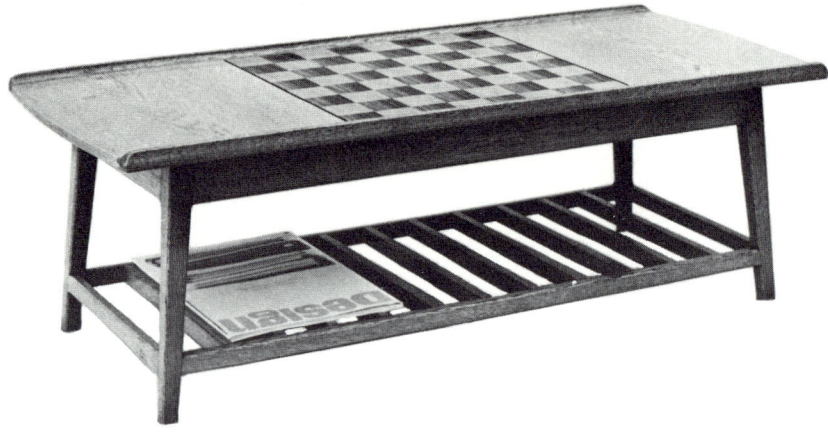

Very suitable for use in a small room.

The limited woods available for dowelling offer no satisfactory blend or contrast with furniture timbers, therefore to obtain an integrated design the type of underframing shown has been employed.

The working drawing shows vertical legs. Will these make the table legs appear safer when used as a seat? It will certainly simplify the construction.

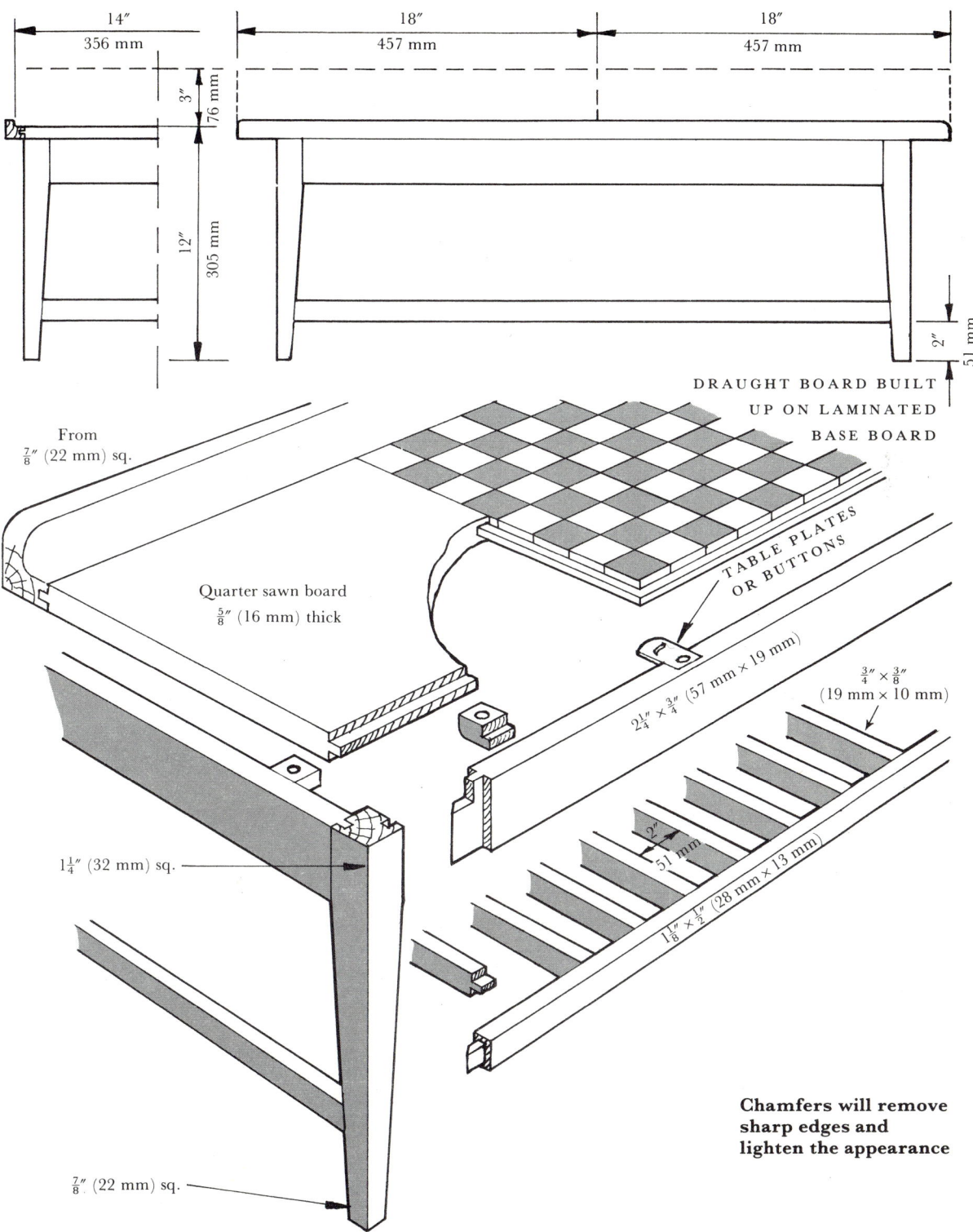

14"
356 mm

18"
457 mm

18"
457 mm

3"
76 mm

12"
305 mm

2"
51 mm

From
$\frac{7}{8}$" (22 mm) sq.

DRAUGHT BOARD BUILT
UP ON LAMINATED
BASE BOARD

Quarter sawn board
$\frac{5}{8}$" (16 mm) thick

TABLE PLATES
OR BUTTONS

$2\frac{1}{4}$" $\times$ $\frac{3}{4}$" (57 mm $\times$ 19 mm)

$\frac{3}{4}$" $\times$ $\frac{3}{8}$"
(19 mm $\times$ 10 mm)

$1\frac{1}{4}$" (32 mm) sq.

2"
51 mm

$1\frac{1}{8}$" $\times$ $\frac{1}{2}$" (28 mm $\times$ 13 mm)

$\frac{7}{8}$" (22 mm) sq.

**Chamfers will remove
sharp edges and
lighten the appearance**

Stool

The frame is made of half inch square section steel tube, with brazed or welded joints, sprayed matt black. The top is natural seagrass.

The sizes suggested on this chart may be useful when designing a stool.

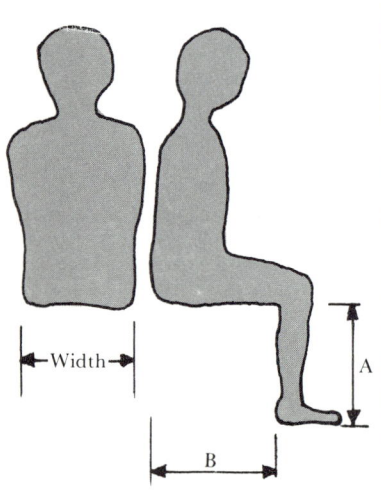

Age	Measurement A	Measurement B	Width
2 Years	7″ 178 mm	8½″ 216 mm	9½″ 242 mm
3 Years	9¼″ 235 mm	10″ 254 mm	9½″ 242 mm
4 Years	10½″ 267 mm	10½″ 267 mm	9½″ 242 mm
5 Years	11½″ 292 mm	12″ 305 mm	10″ 254 mm
6 Years	11½″ 292 mm	12½″ 318 mm	10½″ 267 mm
7 Years	12″ 305 mm	12½″ 318 mm	10½″ 267 mm
8 Years	13″ 330 mm	13″ 330 mm	10½″ 267 mm
9 Years	13½″ 343 mm	14″ 356 mm	11″ 279 mm

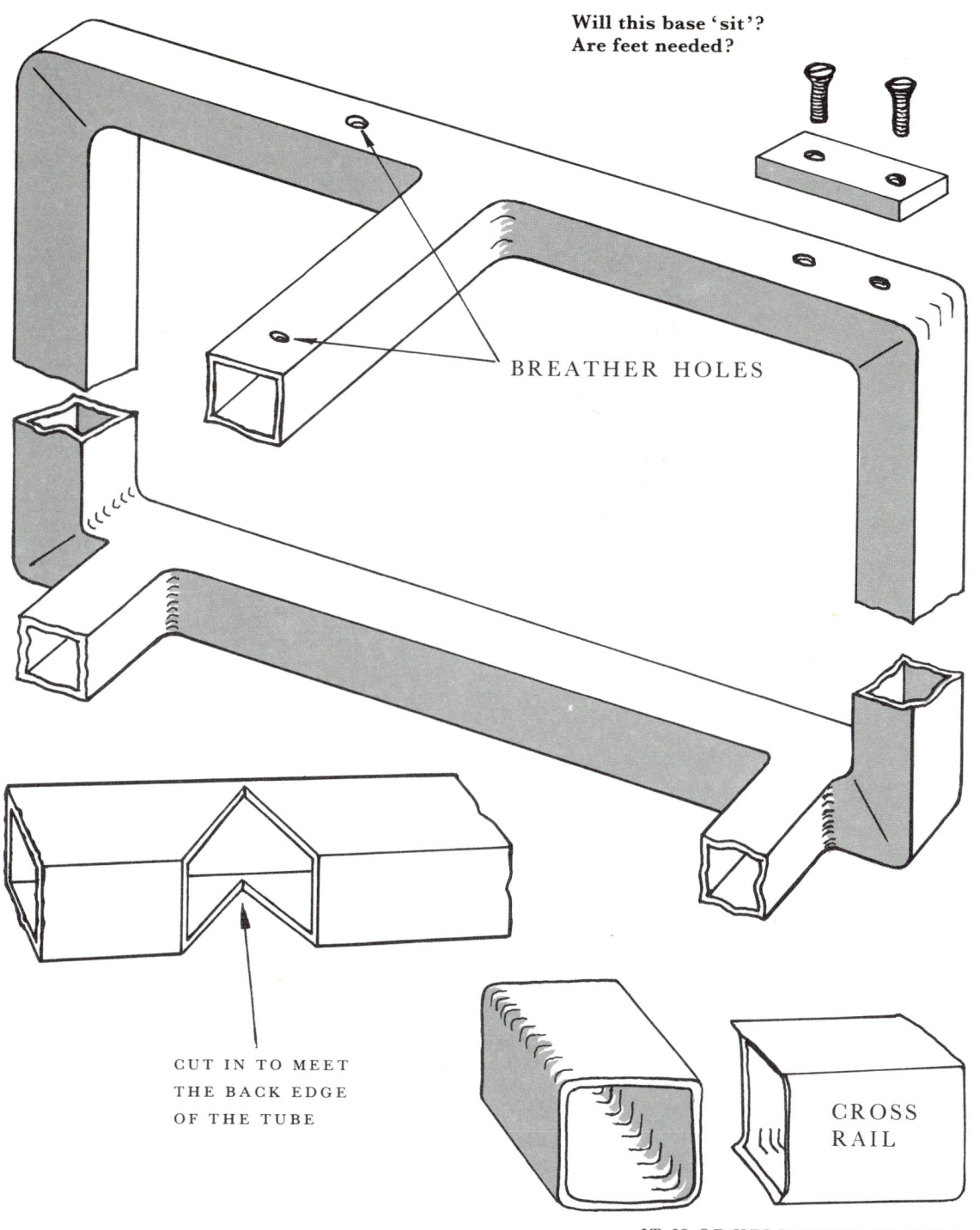

**Will this base 'sit'?
Are feet needed?**

BREATHER HOLES

CUT IN TO MEET
THE BACK EDGE
OF THE TUBE

CROSS
RAIL

IT IS OF HELP WHEN BRAZING,
IF THE CROSSRAIL END IS
SHAPED, AS SHOWN HERE.

Child's stool

In the use of plain mortise and tenon joints, and the woven seat, this article is similar to the chair on page 20.

The staggered top rails and H underframing combine strength with simplicity of construction. The staggered rails also cause the weave to form a curve that adds to the comfort of the seat.

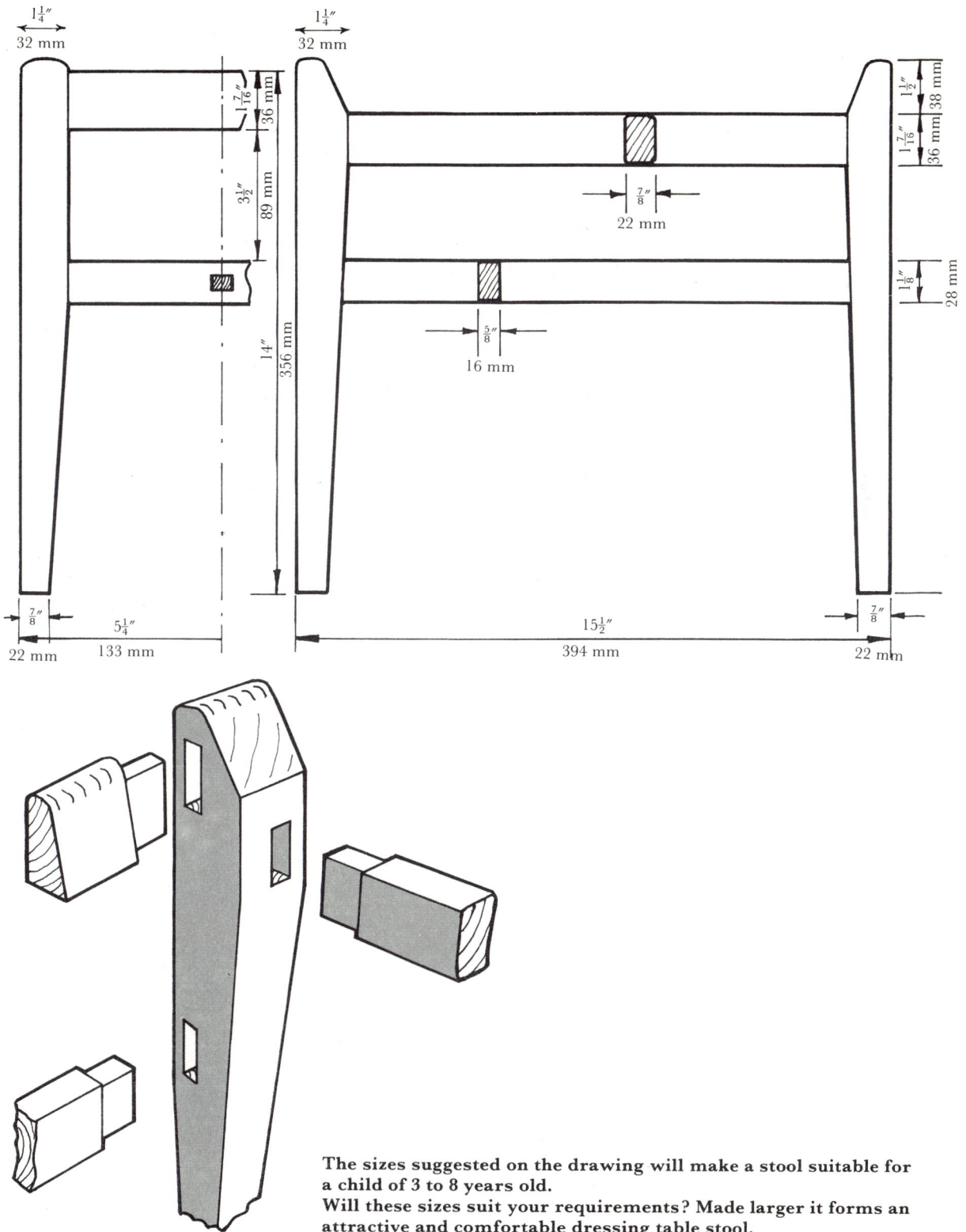

The sizes suggested on the drawing will make a stool suitable for a child of 3 to 8 years old.
Will these sizes suit your requirements? Made larger it forms an attractive and comfortable dressing table stool.

Upholstered stool

This single rail and leg construction is only safe for a stool up to 12″ (305 mm) high. Above this size an additional rail must be placed below. The photograph shows one such arrangement.

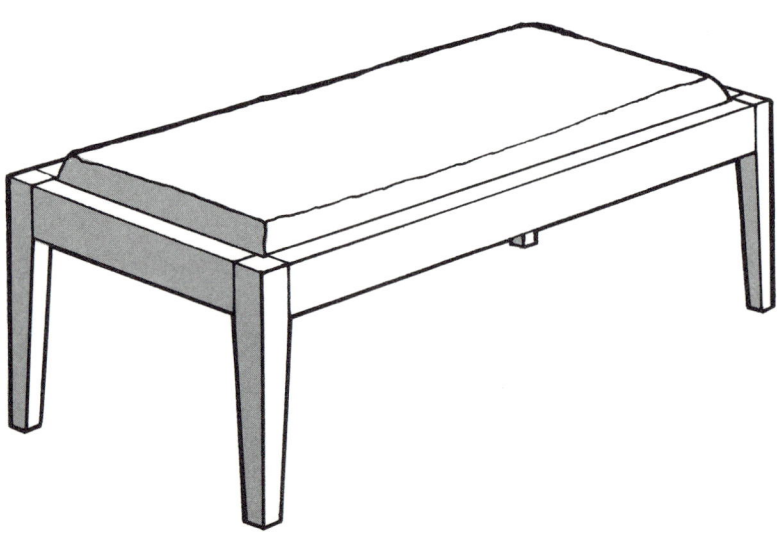

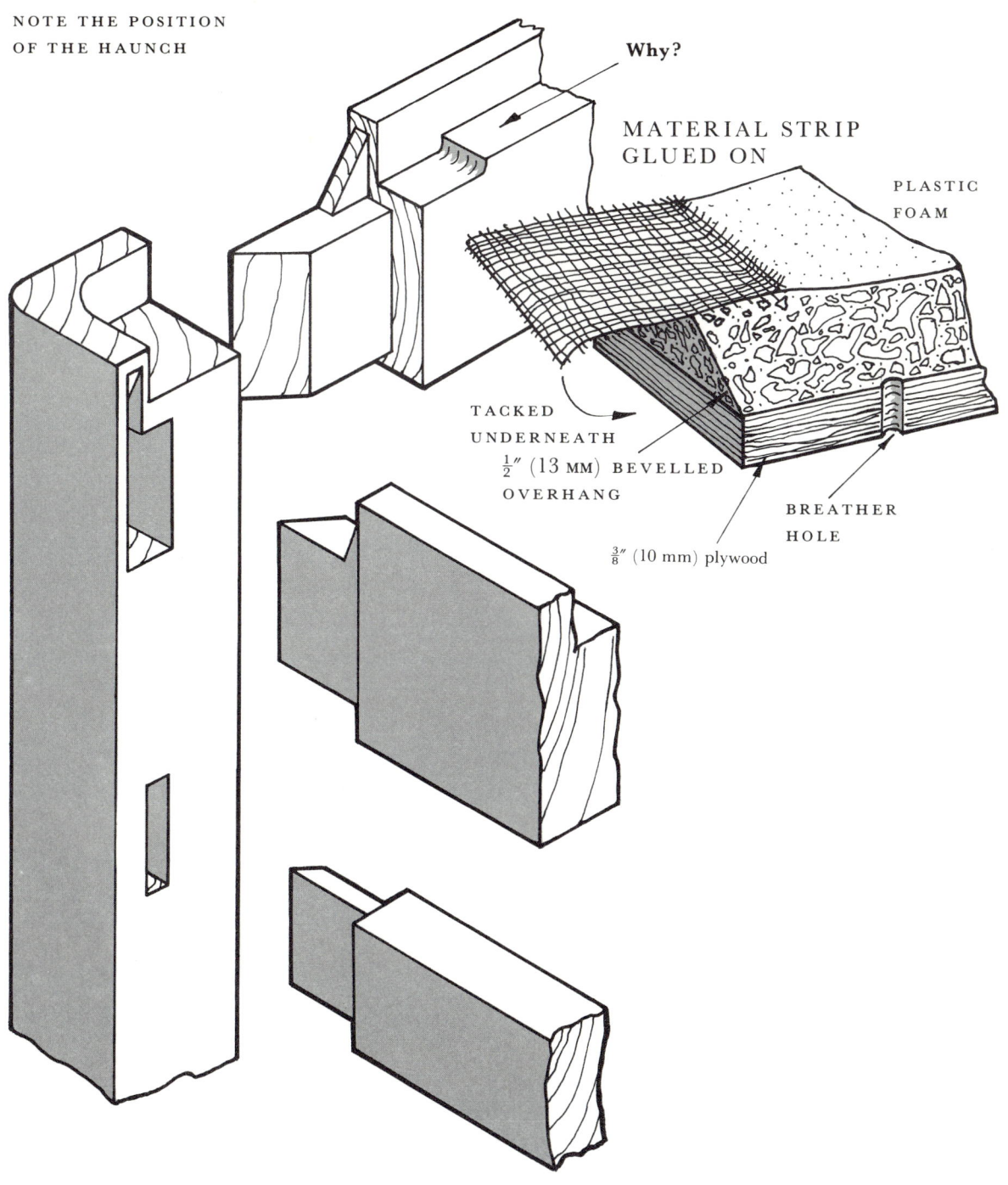

NOTE THE POSITION
OF THE HAUNCH

Why?

MATERIAL STRIP
GLUED ON

PLASTIC
FOAM

TACKED
UNDERNEATH
$\frac{1}{2}''$ (13 mm) BEVELLED
OVERHANG

BREATHER
HOLE

$\frac{3}{8}''$ (10 mm) plywood

Suggested minimum sizes
Legs $1\frac{1}{4}''$ sq. (32 mm)
Top rails $2'' \times \frac{7}{8}''$ (51 mm × 22 mm)
Lower rails $\frac{3}{4}'' \times \frac{1}{2}''$ (19 mm × 13 mm)

Dressing table stool

Using this construction the luxury of upholstery is discarded, but further maintenance is unnecessary.

The split cane used on the end frames adds a pleasing contrast, and it provides for comfortable handling too, but can this be achieved more simply?

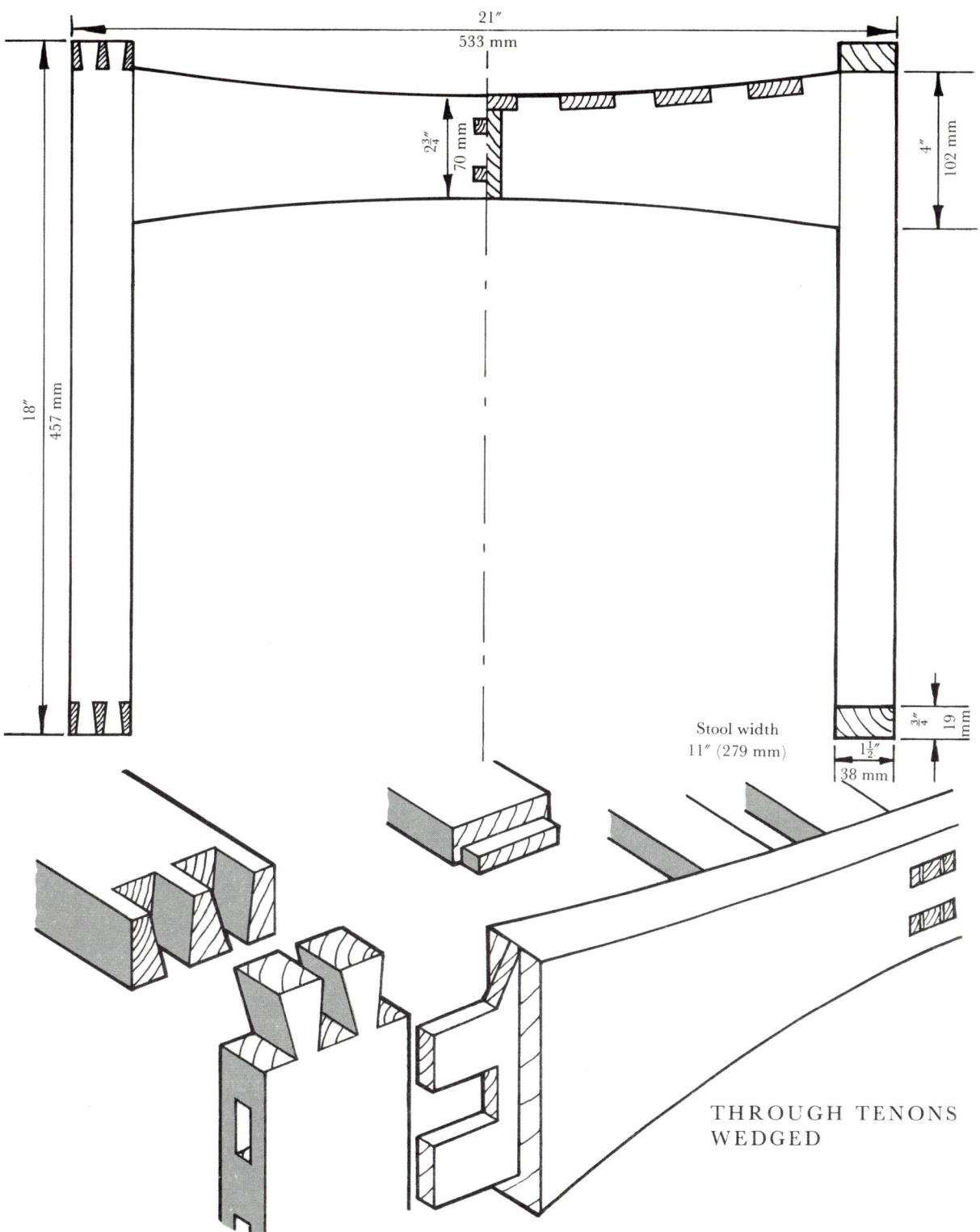

21″
533 mm

2¾″
70 mm

4″
102 mm

18″
457 mm

Stool width
11″ (279 mm)

¾″
19 mm

1½″
38 mm

THROUGH TENONS
WEDGED

Dining chair

In a chair comfort is of first importance, among the critical factors being the height, shape and slope of the back rest.

The laminated back rest here is securely held by glue and brass screws, the screw slots having been filed away, leaving the studs as both functional and decorative features.

The woven seat is comfortable and attractive and strengthens the construction.

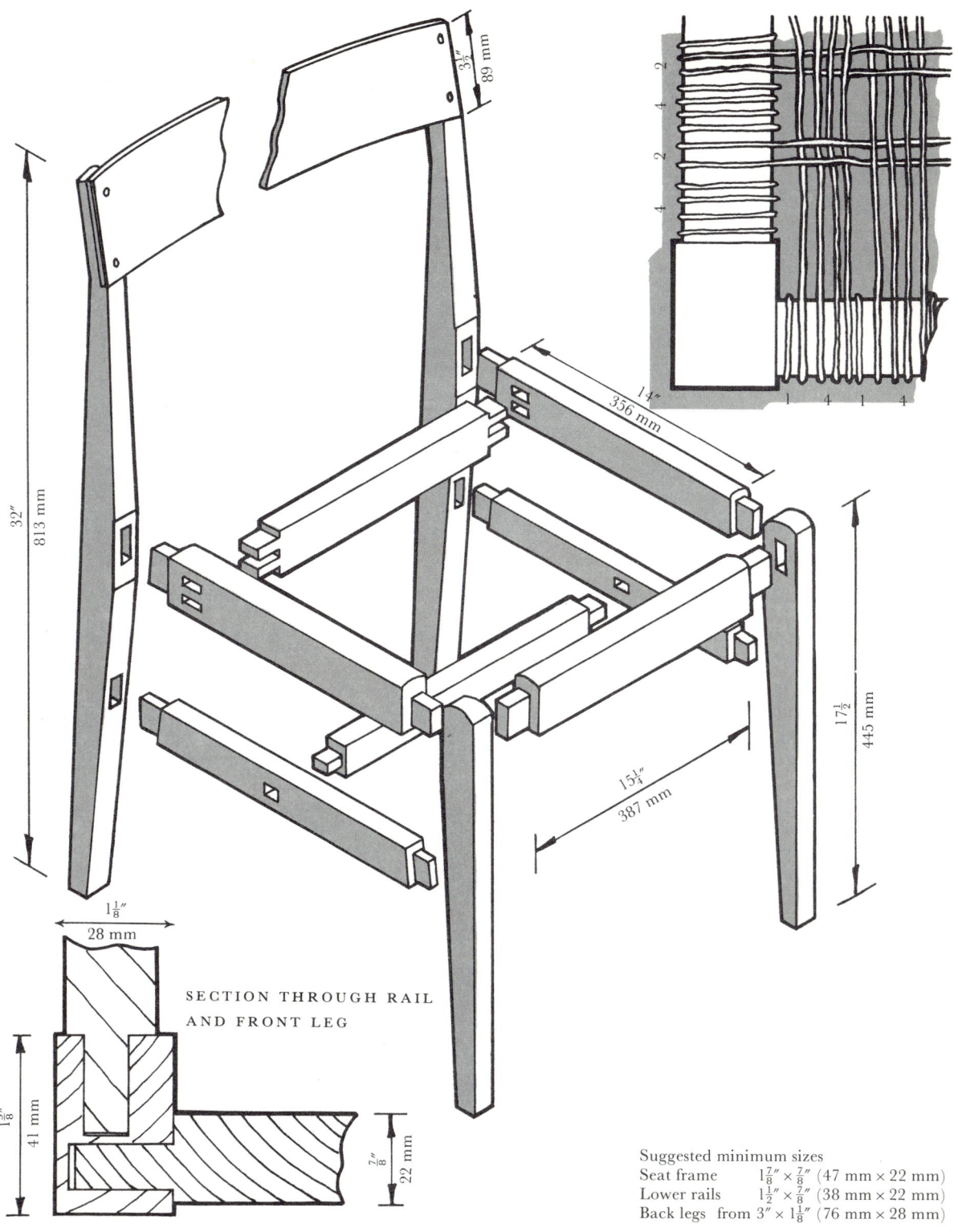

$3\frac{1}{2}''$
89 mm

$32''$
813 mm

$14''$
356 mm

$17\frac{1}{2}$
445 mm

$15\frac{1}{4}''$
387 mm

$1\frac{1}{8}''$
28 mm

$1\frac{5}{8}''$
41 mm

$\frac{7}{8}''$
22 mm

2 4 2 4

1 4 1 4

SECTION THROUGH RAIL
AND FRONT LEG

Suggested minimum sizes
Seat frame $1\frac{7}{8}'' \times \frac{7}{8}''$ (47 mm × 22 mm)
Lower rails $1\frac{1}{2}'' \times \frac{7}{8}''$ (38 mm × 22 mm)
Back legs from $3'' \times 1\frac{1}{8}''$ (76 mm × 28 mm)

Dining table

The idea is adapted from a Sheraton card table (antiques provide an abundance of ideas).
Made for use in a small room. The simple swivel folding top with this construction allows space for chairs when not in use.

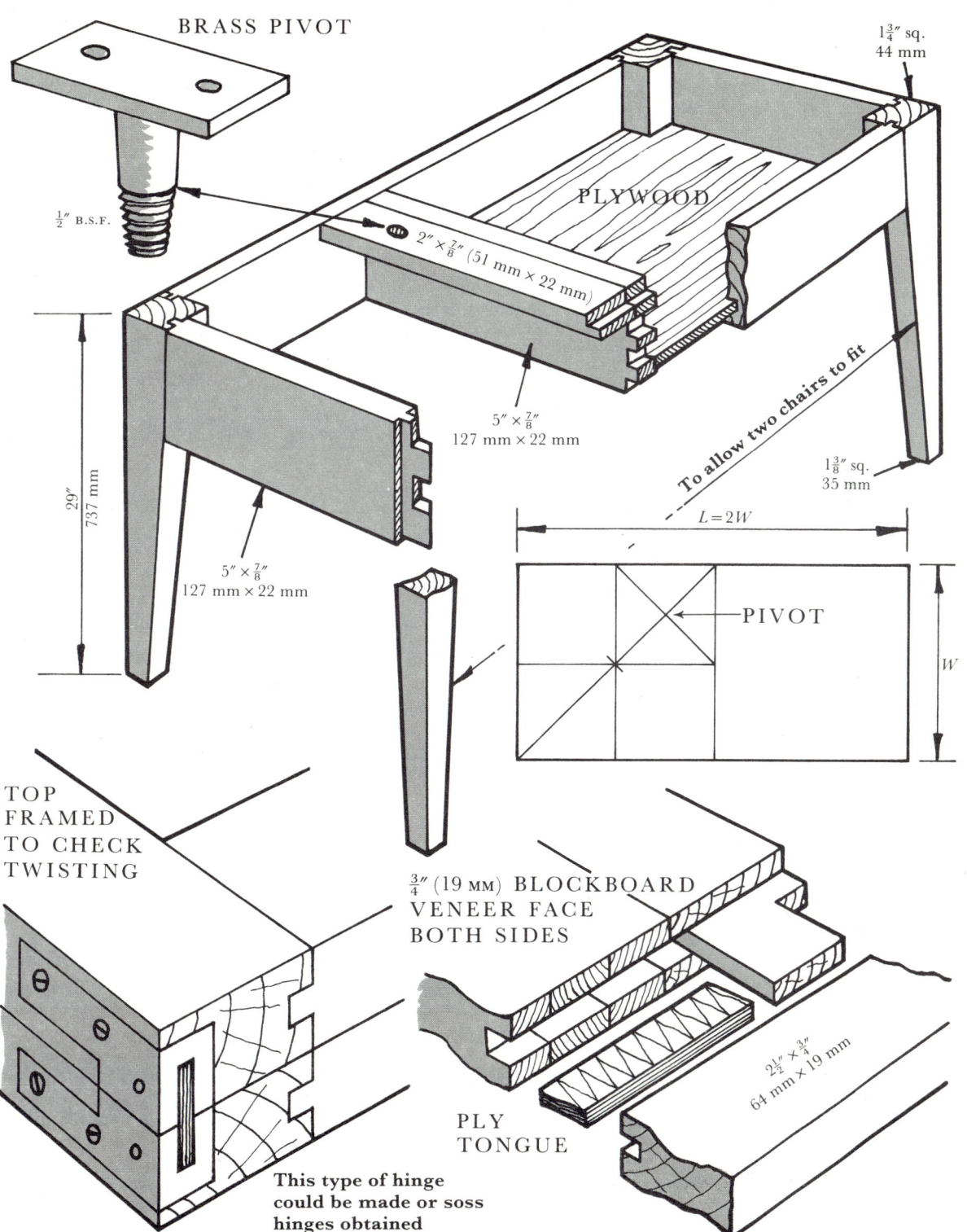

BRASS PIVOT

$\frac{1}{2}''$ B.S.F.

$1\frac{3}{4}''$ sq.
44 mm

PLYWOOD

$2'' \times \frac{7}{8}''$ $(51\ mm \times 22\ mm)$

To allow two chairs to fit

$5'' \times \frac{7}{8}''$
127 mm × 22 mm

$1\frac{3}{8}''$ sq.
35 mm

29"
737 mm

$5'' \times \frac{7}{8}''$
127 mm × 22 mm

$L = 2W$

PIVOT

W

TOP
FRAMED
TO CHECK
TWISTING

$\frac{3}{4}''$ (19 ᴍᴍ) BLOCKBOARD
VENEER FACE
BOTH SIDES

$2\frac{1}{2}'' \times \frac{3}{4}''$
64 mm × 19 mm

PLY
TONGUE

This type of hinge
could be made or soss
hinges obtained

Bookcase

A depth of 7″ (178 mm) is adequate for bookshelves but insufficient for a cupboard. This combined design was aimed at avoiding a compromise.

Boards of English Oak, quarter sawn, were carefully selected for this piece as they reveal the beauty of their silver grain. Is the decoration provided by the functional through dovetails compatible with this natural beauty?

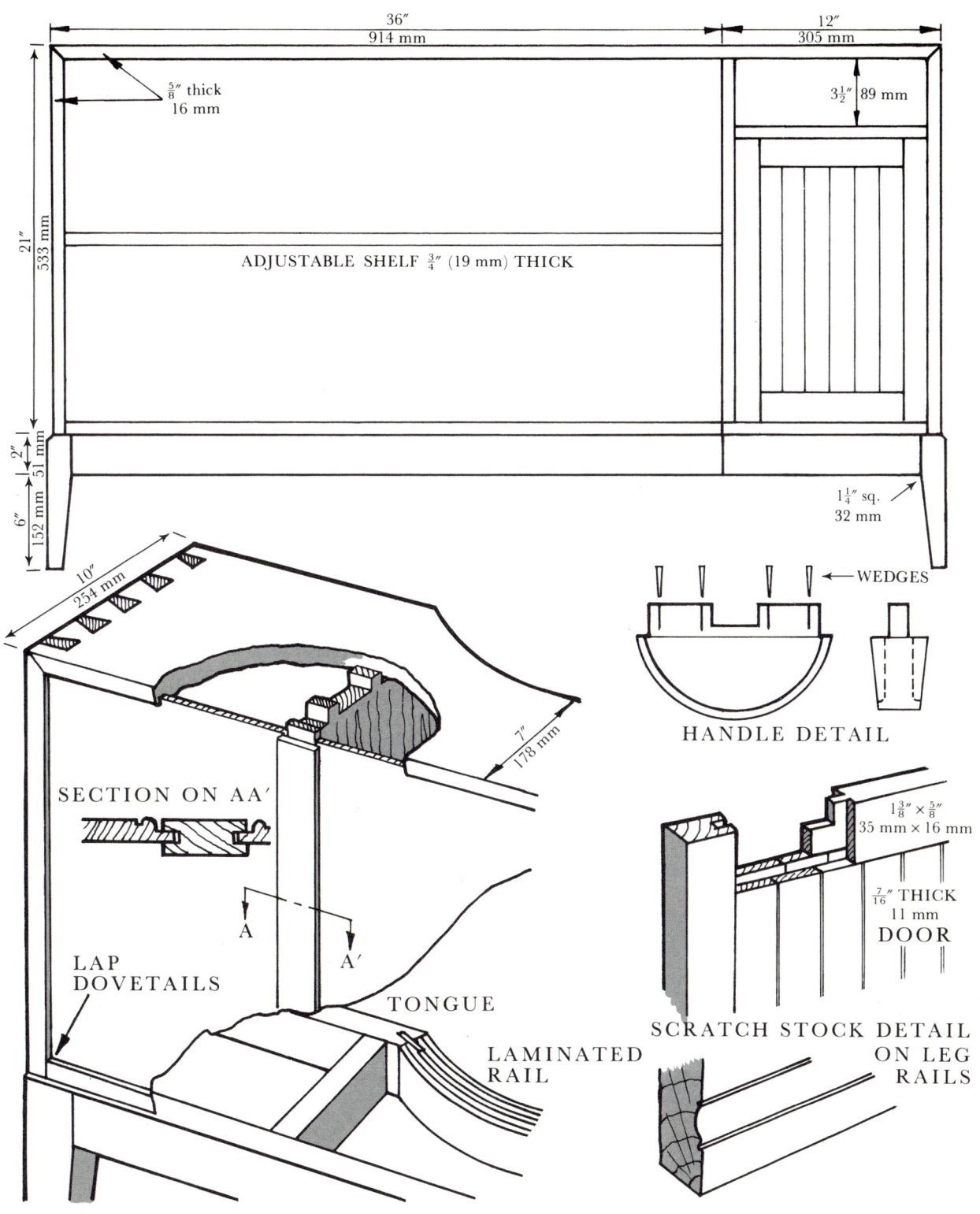

36"
914 mm

12"
305 mm

5⁄8" thick
16 mm

3½" | 89 mm

21"
533 mm

ADJUSTABLE SHELF ¾" (19 mm) THICK

2"
51 mm

6"
152 mm

1¼" sq.
32 mm

10"
254 mm

7"
178 mm

SECTION ON AA'

A

A'

LAP
DOVETAILS

TONGUE

LAMINATED
RAIL

WEDGES

HANDLE DETAIL

1⅜" × 5⁄8"
35 mm × 16 mm

7⁄16" THICK
11 mm
DOOR

SCRATCH STOCK DETAIL
ON LEG
RAILS

3

Wall bookshelves

Adequate wall space allowed freedom of dimensions but the shelves were built to accommodate specific book sizes. The length of the shelves was related to the height and the rectangle then formed suggested the proportions of the cupboard and consequently the whole unit.

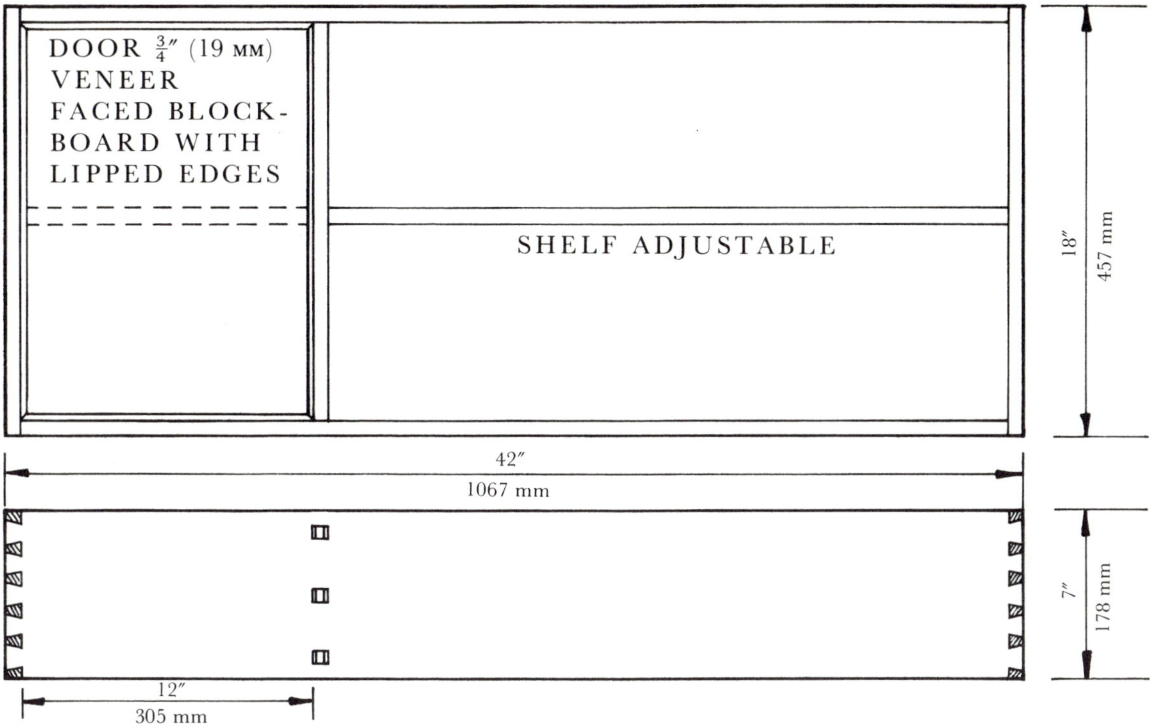

DOOR $\frac{3}{4}''$ (19 ΜΜ) VENEER FACED BLOCK- BOARD WITH LIPPED EDGES

SHELF ADJUSTABLE

18"
457 mm

42"
1067 mm

7"
178 mm

12"
305 mm

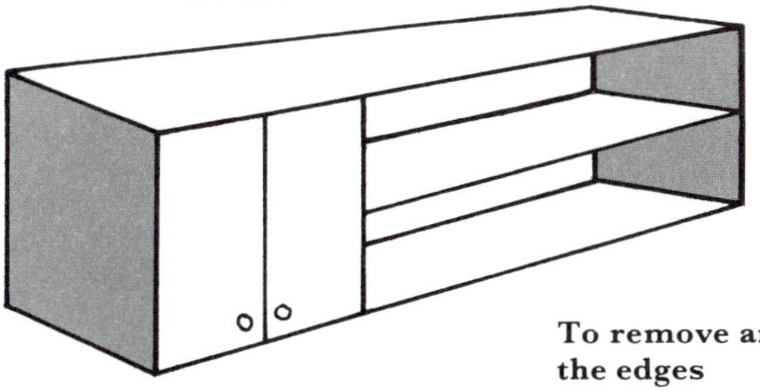

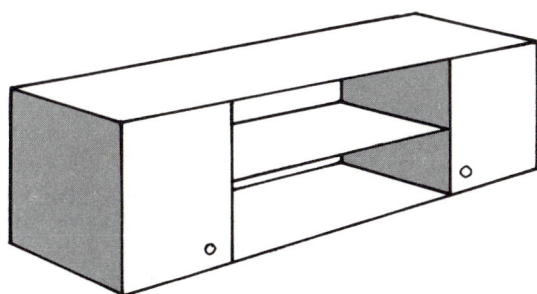

To remove any sharpness and to lighten the appearance, chamfer the edges

Are these shelf sizes adequate for your books?

Is a plywood back considered necessary? If so what type of dovetail joint is needed to allow for a rebated back edge?

The door could be of a framed construction as on page 25

Would a shelf inside the cupboard be useful? Adjustable?

Record cupboard

The cupboard sizes have been controlled by the dimensions of record sleeves—not the record! Compare the wall fixing with that on page 36, necessary because of the weight.

The doors of balanced hardboard ensuring a flat surface, have thin strip handles, these allow the doors to slide past each other. Alternative door arrangements might be considered according to circumstances of space and position.

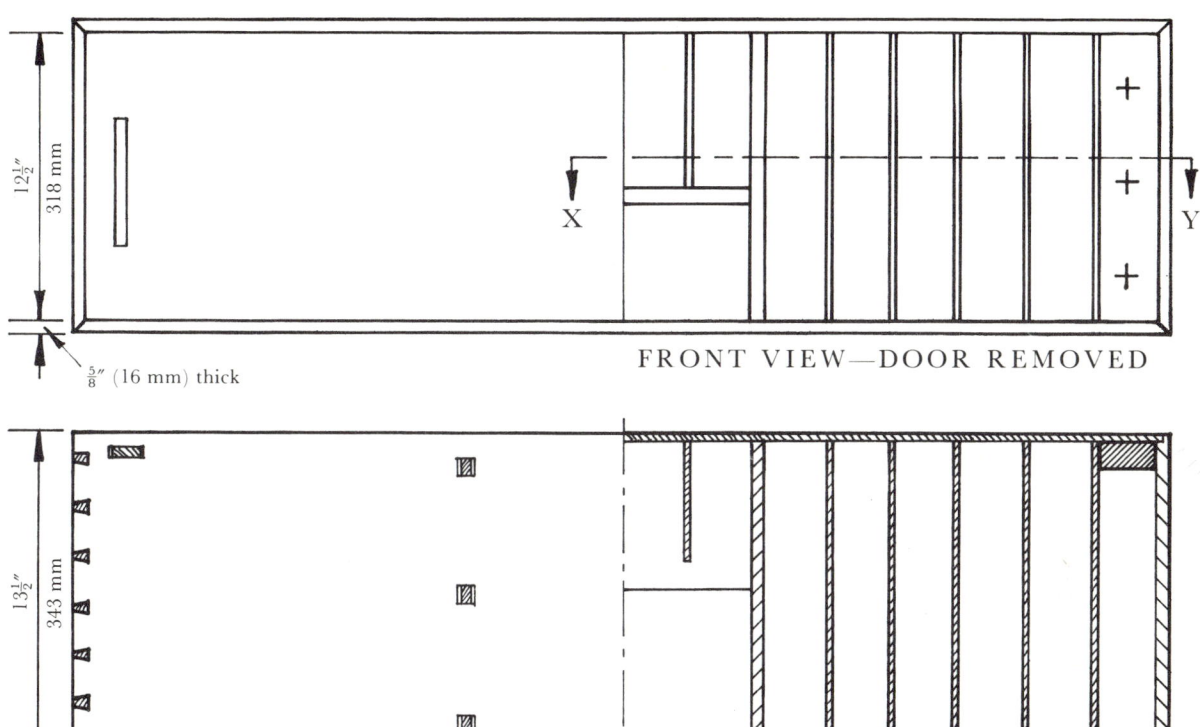

$12\frac{1}{2}''$
318 mm

$\frac{5}{8}''$ (16 mm) thick

FRONT VIEW—DOOR REMOVED

$13\frac{1}{2}''$
343 mm

PLAN—SECTIONAL ON XY

PLYWOOD BACK—
REBATED EDGES

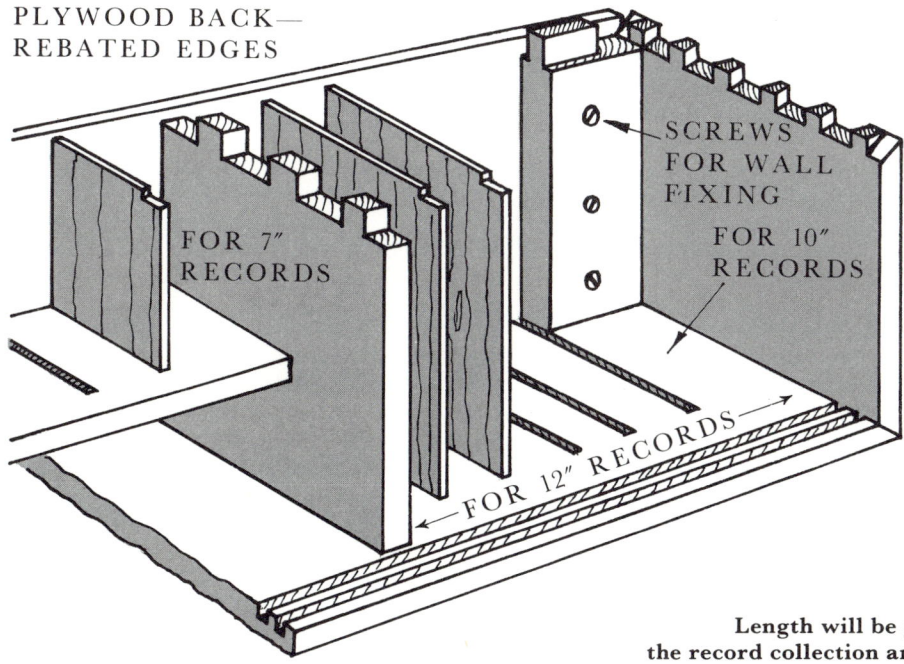

FOR 7"
RECORDS

SCREWS
FOR WALL
FIXING

FOR 10"
RECORDS

FOR 12" RECORDS

**Length will be governed by the size of
the record collection and available wall space**

Record rack

The use of wood and metal allows a simple construction.
The width has been carefully chosen to allow 7″ records to be held
with or without their sleeves.

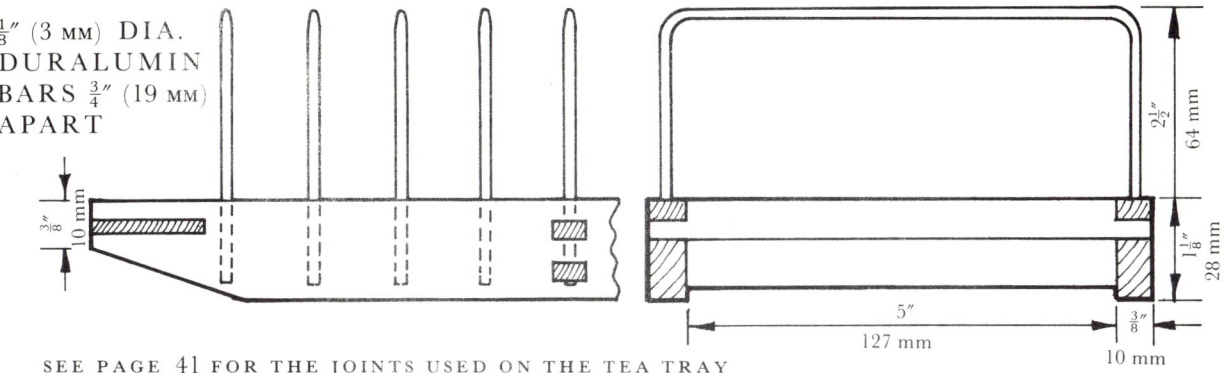

$\frac{1}{8}''$ (3 mm) DIA.
DURALUMIN
BARS $\frac{3}{4}''$ (19 mm)
APART

$\frac{3}{8}''$ 10 mm

$2\frac{1}{2}''$ 64 mm

$1\frac{1}{8}''$ 28 mm

5" 127 mm

$\frac{3}{8}''$ 10 mm

SEE PAGE 41 FOR THE JOINTS USED ON THE TEA TRAY

The length of the rack will depend on individual requirements

Is this type of rack useful for 12″ dia. records or is a cupboard more suitable?

Toast racks?

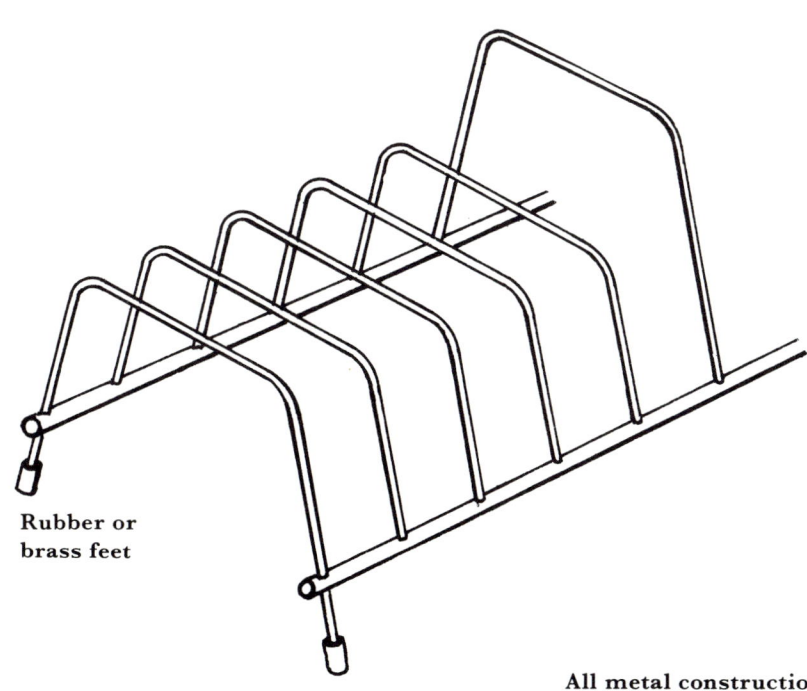

Rubber or
brass feet

All metal construction?

What metal, joints, and finish could be used?

Will you use a jig when bending the bars to shape?

Record rack 31

Magazine rack

The vertically arranged dividing bars will allow easy insertion of papers and magazines from the top, while the flat strips used for the feet provide stability.

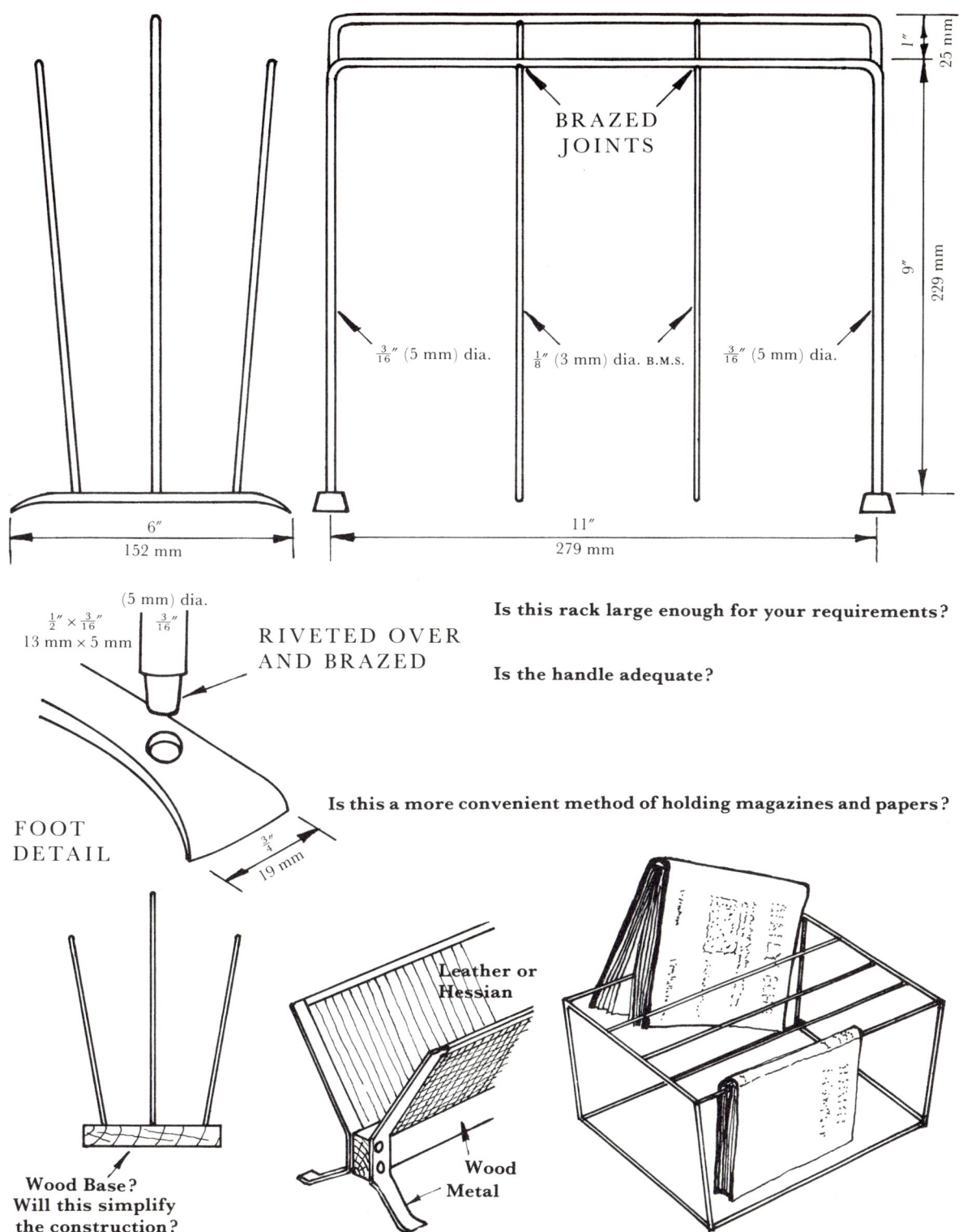

BRAZED JOINTS

$\frac{3}{16}''$ (5 mm) dia.　$\frac{1}{8}''$ (3 mm) dia. B.M.S.　$\frac{3}{16}''$ (5 mm) dia.

1" 25 mm

9" 229 mm

6" 152 mm

11" 279 mm

(5 mm) dia.

$\frac{1}{2}'' \times \frac{3}{16}''$
13 mm × 5 mm

$\frac{3}{16}''$

RIVETED OVER AND BRAZED

FOOT DETAIL

$\frac{3}{4}''$ 19 mm

Is this rack large enough for your requirements?

Is the handle adequate?

Is this a more convenient method of holding magazines and papers?

Wood Base?
Will this simplify
the construction?

Leather or Hessian

Wood
Metal

Bathroom cupboard

A bathroom cupboard must be easily accessible to adults, yet must not be a danger to the head being raised from that basin. This being so the cupboards here are only 5″ (127 mm) deep. The shelves are covered with plastic laminate for hygienic reasons. The mirror between the cupboards is tilted forward to enable it to be used by both adults and children.

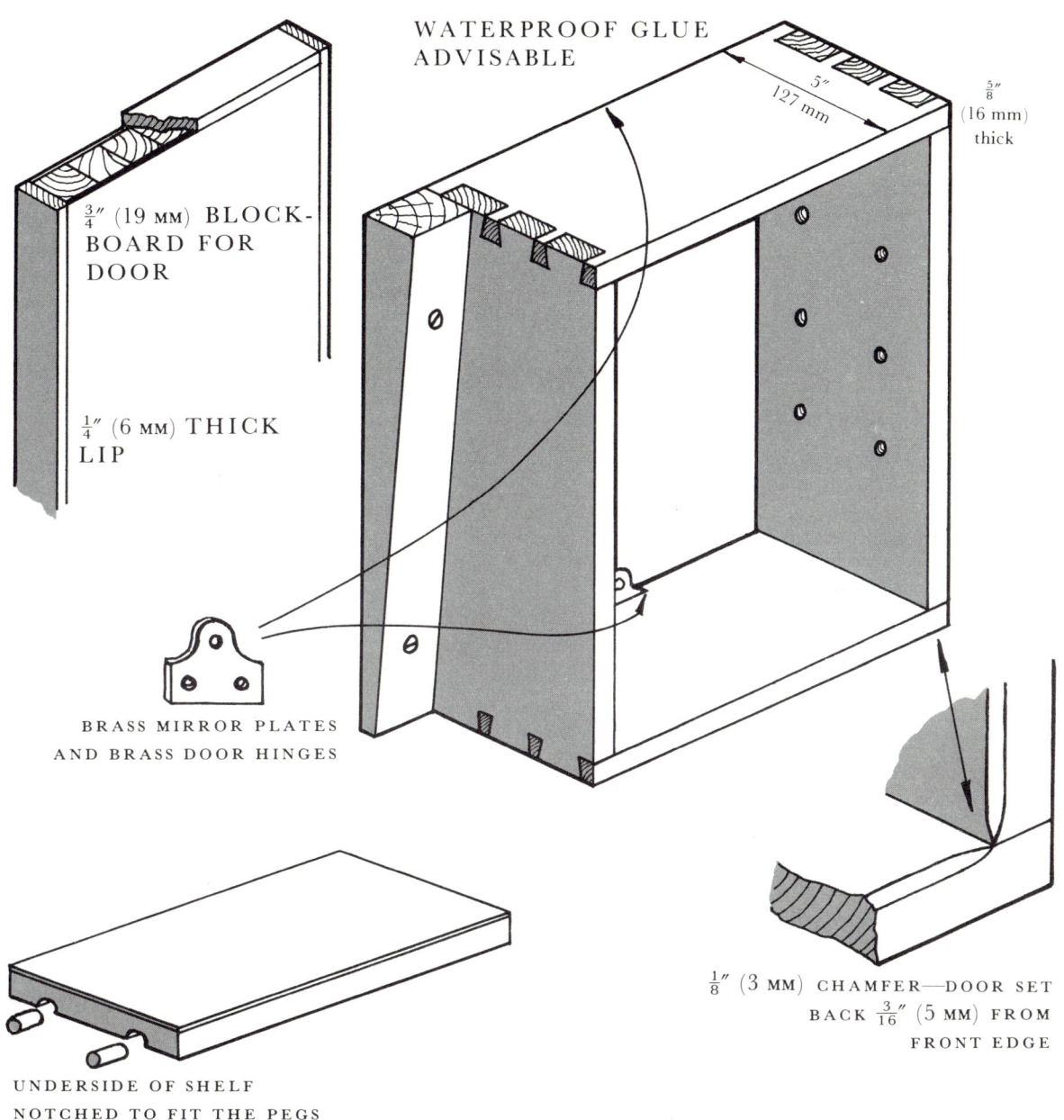

WATERPROOF GLUE
ADVISABLE

$\frac{3}{4}''$ (19 MM) BLOCK-
BOARD FOR
DOOR

$\frac{1}{4}''$ (6 MM) THICK
LIP

5"
127 mm

$\frac{5}{8}''$
(16 mm)
thick

BRASS MIRROR PLATES
AND BRASS DOOR HINGES

UNDERSIDE OF SHELF
NOTCHED TO FIT THE PEGS
USED FOR SHELF ADJUSTMENT

$\frac{1}{8}''$ (3 MM) CHAMFER—DOOR SET
BACK $\frac{3}{16}''$ (5 MM) FROM
FRONT EDGE

**A list of things to be kept in these cupboards helps to determine
overall sizes**

Standard mirror sizes?

Is a lock necessary?

Kitchen cupboards

Items less frequently used in the kitchen are kept in this cupboard, which is fixed to the ceiling and the top of a glazed screen between eating and cooking areas.

Electric meters are enclosed in the upper part of this cupboard, the lower part allowing for food storage at a convenient height.
The width of 10″ (254 mm) accommodates large cereal packets and the height of a shelf inside is adjustable.
The grain and colour of the yellow deal, the through joints and the clear polyurethane finish overcome the clinical appearance of most kitchen furniture.

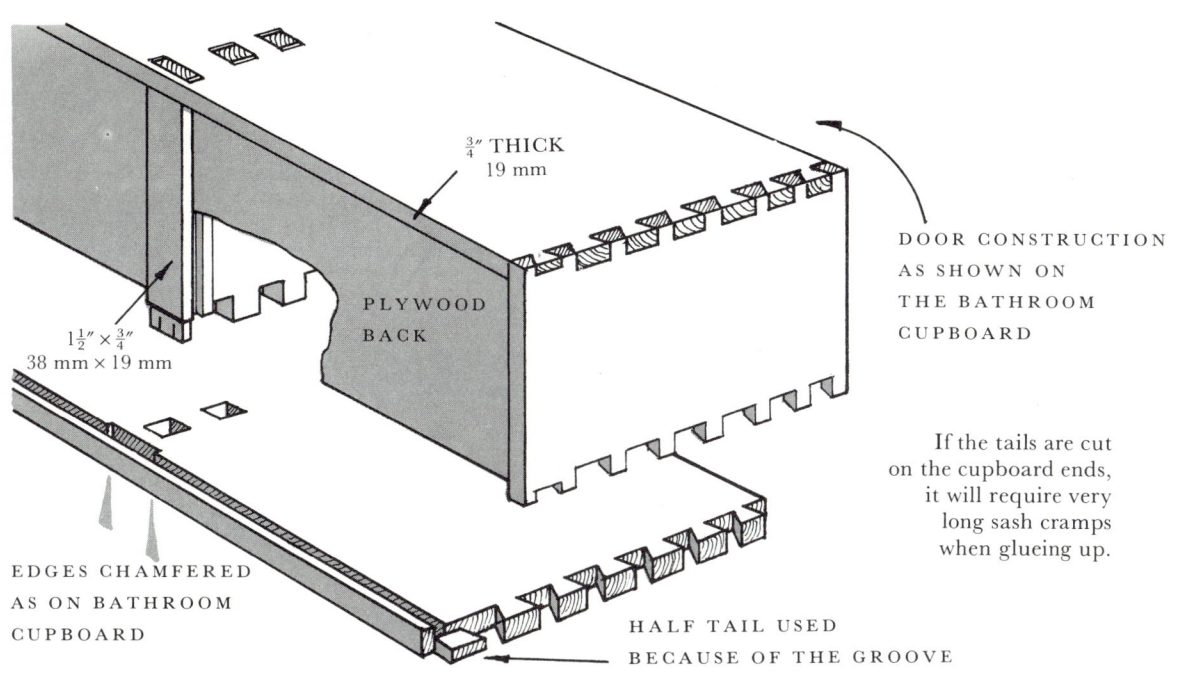

$\frac{3}{4}''$ THICK
19 mm

PLYWOOD
BACK

$1\frac{1}{2}'' \times \frac{3}{4}''$
38 mm × 19 mm

EDGES CHAMFERED
AS ON BATHROOM
CUPBOARD

HALF TAIL USED
BECAUSE OF THE GROOVE

DOOR CONSTRUCTION
AS SHOWN ON
THE BATHROOM
CUPBOARD

If the tails are cut
on the cupboard ends,
it will require very
long sash cramps
when glueing up.

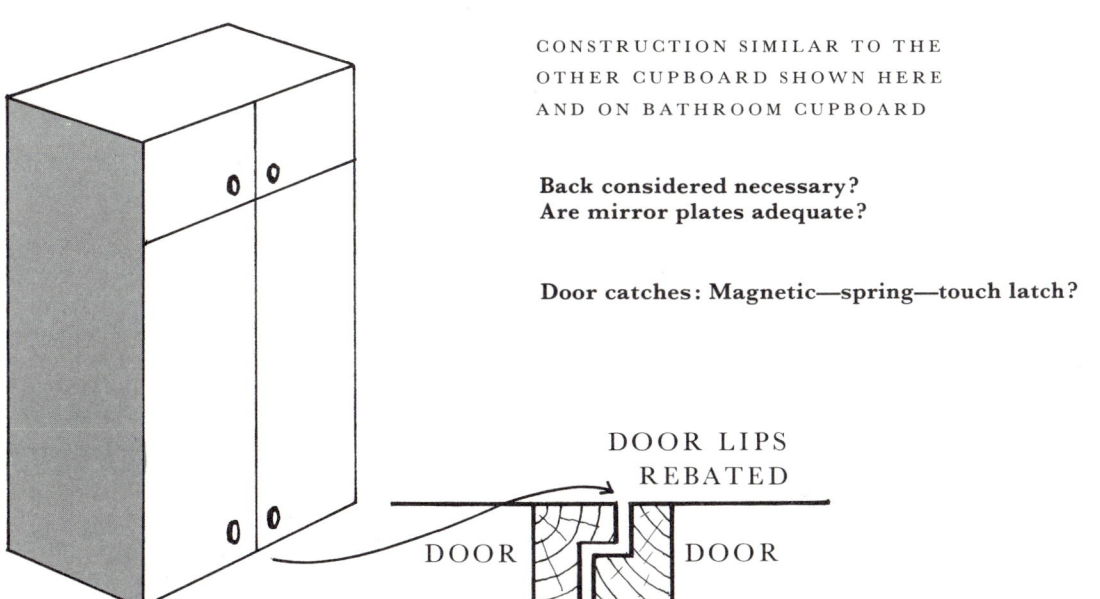

CONSTRUCTION SIMILAR TO THE
OTHER CUPBOARD SHOWN HERE
AND ON BATHROOM CUPBOARD

**Back considered necessary?
Are mirror plates adequate?**

Door catches: Magnetic—spring—touch latch?

DOOR LIPS
REBATED

DOOR   DOOR

Dressing table

Similar to the kitchen cupboard, but using polished mahogany. A decorative plastic laminate is used on the top as it provides a surface that can be easily cleaned of cosmetics.

The choice of a neutral colour for this top avoids a clash with any future colour scheme.

Kitchen cupboard

A cupboard for food and a large working top next to the refrigerator and below the food cupboard shown on the previous page. The cooker and wall scales are conveniently placed.

The depth of the cupboard is such that the handles of the cooker and refrigerator do not protrude and the cupboard drawer and door handles are shaped to avoid any projection. Wood and finish are the same as those used for the wall cupboard.

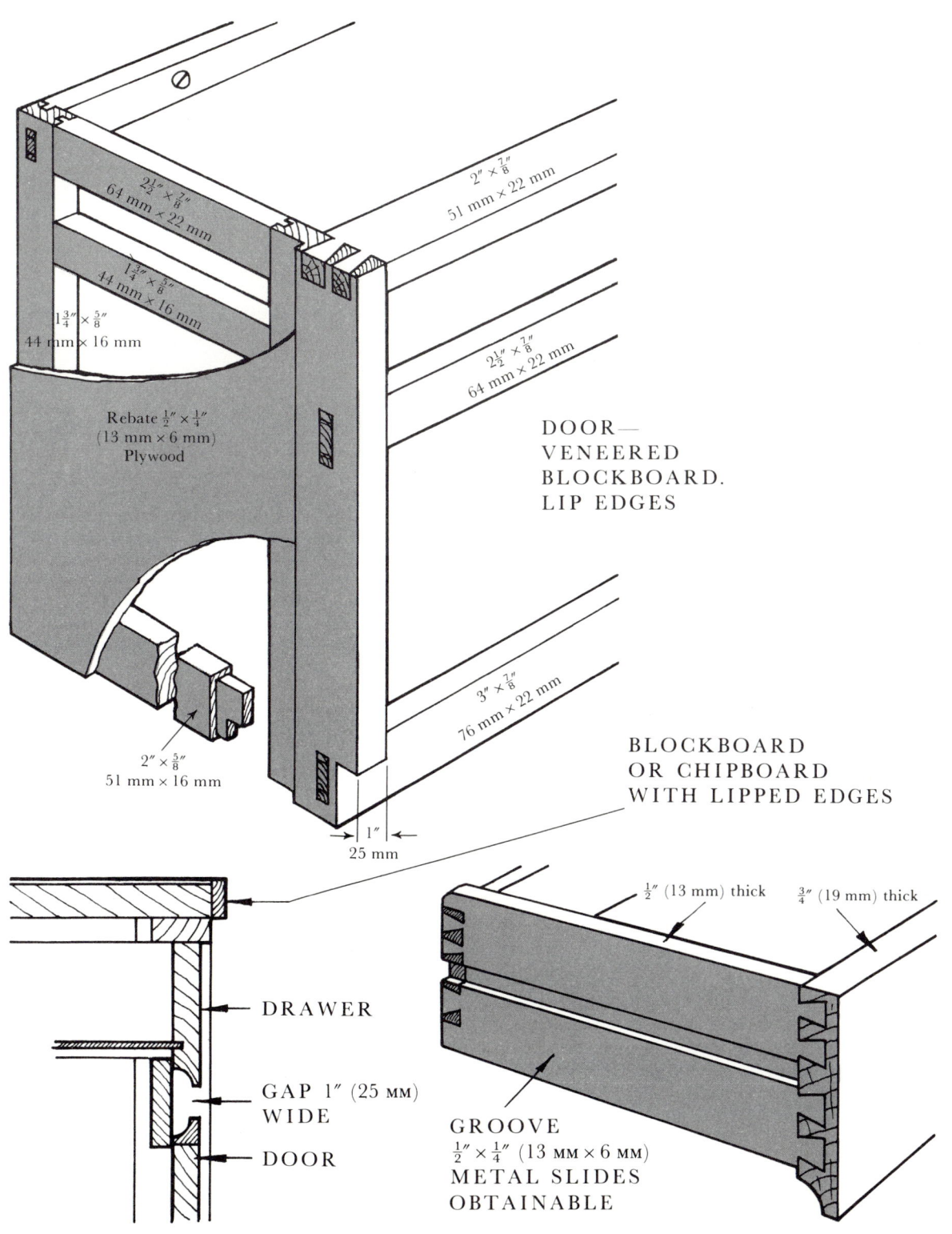

$2\frac{1}{2}'' \times \frac{7}{8}''$
64 mm × 22 mm

$1\frac{3}{4}'' \times \frac{5}{8}''$
44 mm × 16 mm

$1\frac{3}{4}'' \times \frac{5}{8}''$
44 mm × 16 mm

$2'' \times \frac{7}{8}''$
51 mm × 22 mm

$2\frac{1}{2}'' \times \frac{7}{8}''$
64 mm × 22 mm

Rebate $\frac{1}{2}'' \times \frac{1}{4}''$
(13 mm × 6 mm)
Plywood

DOOR—
VENEERED
BLOCKBOARD.
LIP EDGES

$3'' \times \frac{7}{8}''$
76 mm × 22 mm

BLOCKBOARD
OR CHIPBOARD
WITH LIPPED EDGES

$2'' \times \frac{5}{8}''$
51 mm × 16 mm

$1''$
25 mm

$\frac{1}{2}''$ (13 mm) thick

$\frac{3}{4}''$ (19 mm) thick

DRAWER

GAP 1" (25 мм)
WIDE

DOOR

GROOVE
$\frac{1}{2}'' \times \frac{1}{4}''$ (13 мм × 6 мм)
METAL SLIDES
OBTAINABLE

Dressing table   Kitchen cupboard   39

Tea tray

This tray, large enough to hold six saucers and so of a size that is generally useful, is light, simple, yet of a strong construction.

The handles are efficient and leave the ends open to allow easy cleaning. (These open ends are not so large that plates or saucers will slip through.)

The plastic laminate base is not only hygienic but can provide a pleasing contrast to the wood.

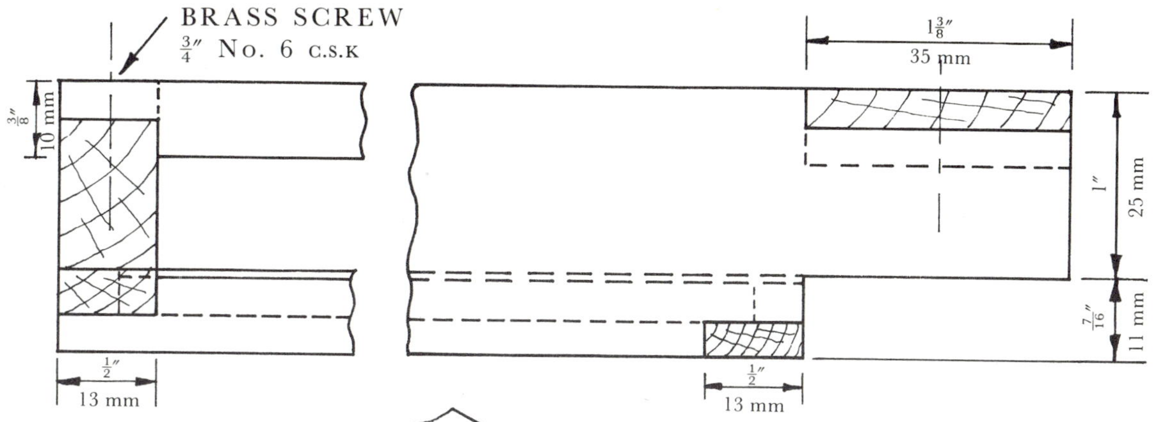

BRASS SCREW
$\frac{3}{4}''$ No. 6 c.s.k

$\frac{3}{8}''$ 10 mm

$1\frac{3}{8}''$
35 mm

1" 25 mm

$\frac{7}{16}''$ 11 mm

$\frac{1}{2}''$
13 mm

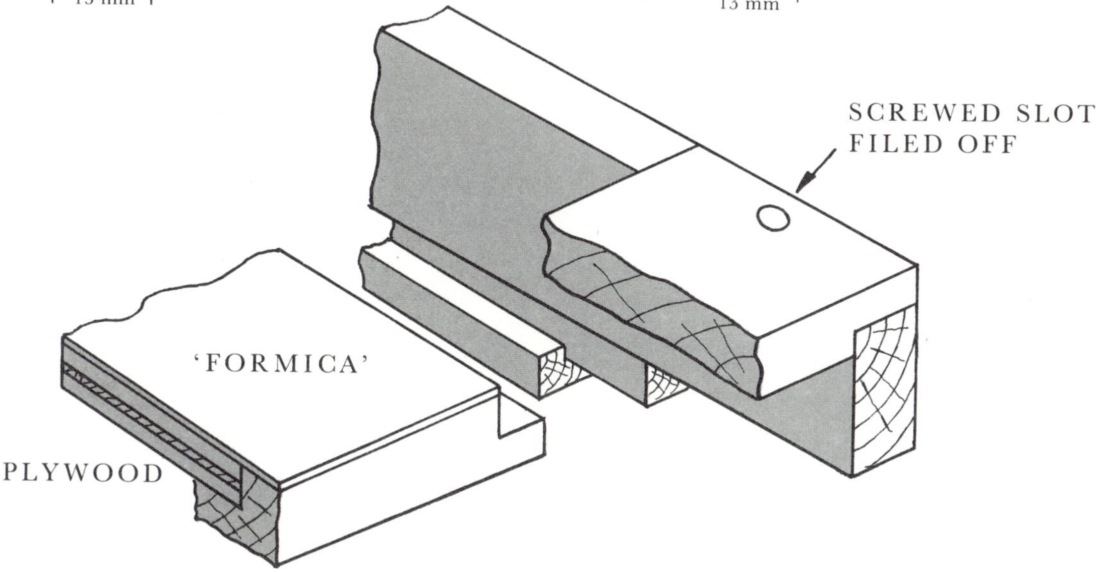

$\frac{1}{2}''$
13 mm

SCREWED SLOT
FILED OFF

'FORMICA'

PLYWOOD

ALTERNATIVE
JOINT

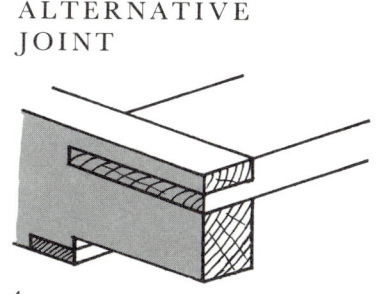

Overall Sizes?

Base 12″ × 18″ (305 mm × 457 mm)

Is this a suitable size for your household?

4

Tea strainer

Nickel silver is hygienic, wood is a poor conductor of heat, and together these materials provide a pleasing contrast.
The triangular shape ensures a firm seating on the cup.
The piercing of the bowl is arranged along radial lines and so becomes decorative. The rivets also are both functional and decorative.

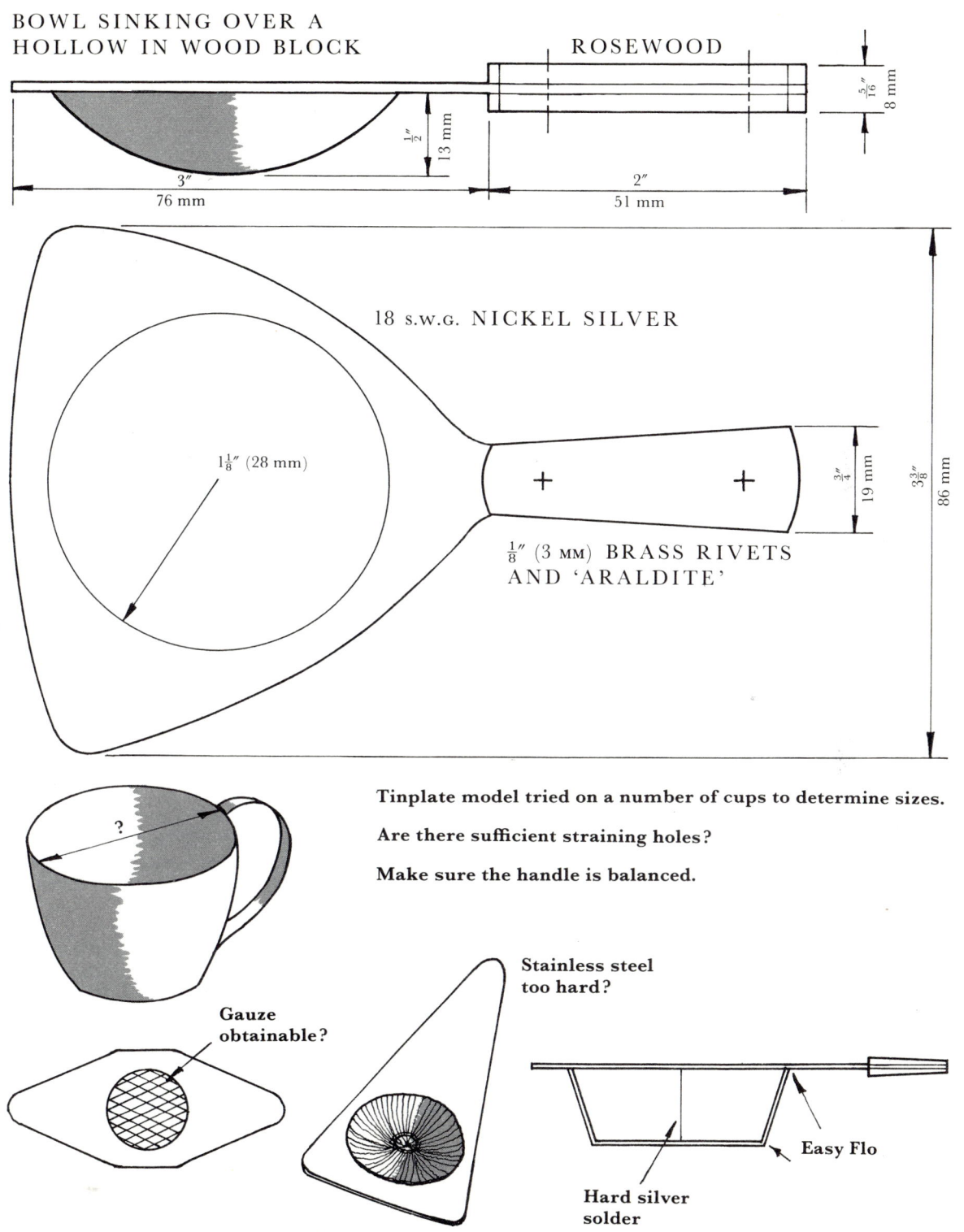

BOWL SINKING OVER A
HOLLOW IN WOOD BLOCK

ROSEWOOD

$\frac{5}{16}''$ 8 mm

$\frac{1}{2}''$ 13 mm

3″ 76 mm

2″ 51 mm

18 s.w.g. NICKEL SILVER

$1\frac{1}{8}''$ (28 mm)

$\frac{1}{8}''$ (3 MM) BRASS RIVETS
AND 'ARALDITE'

$\frac{3}{4}''$ 19 mm

$3\frac{3}{8}''$ 86 mm

Tinplate model tried on a number of cups to determine sizes.

Are there sufficient straining holes?

Make sure the handle is balanced.

?

Stainless steel
too hard?

Gauze
obtainable?

Hard silver
solder

Easy Flo

Egg cups

Part of a jug being made in the workshop suggested this shape as an egg cup. An advantage is that it allows a number of the articles to be stacked.

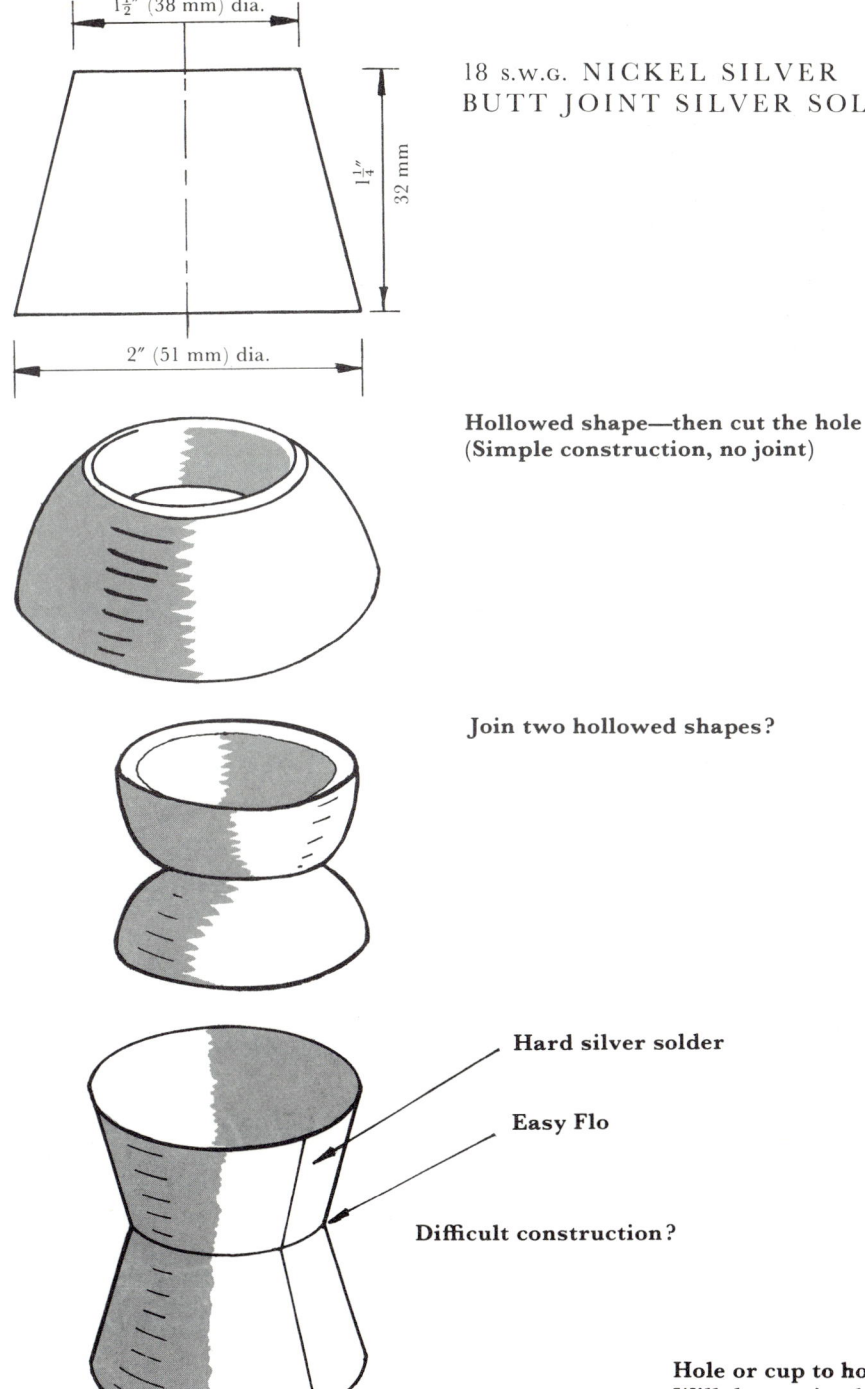

1½″ (38 mm) dia.

1¼″ 32 mm

2″ (51 mm) dia.

18 s.w.g. NICKEL SILVER
BUTT JOINT SILVER SOLDERED

Hollowed shape—then cut the hole
(Simple construction, no joint)

Join two hollowed shapes?

Hard silver solder

Easy Flo

Difficult construction?

Hole or cup to hold the egg?
Will decoration harbour dirt?
Can the empty egg shell be easily removed?
Will the shape allow stacking?

Egg cups 45

Milk jugs

$2\frac{1}{4}''$ (57 mm) dia. $1\frac{1}{4}''$ 32 mm

1 **Nickel silver—
a hard metal to raise**

2 **Gilding metal—
needs plating**

3 **Sterling silver—
expensive**

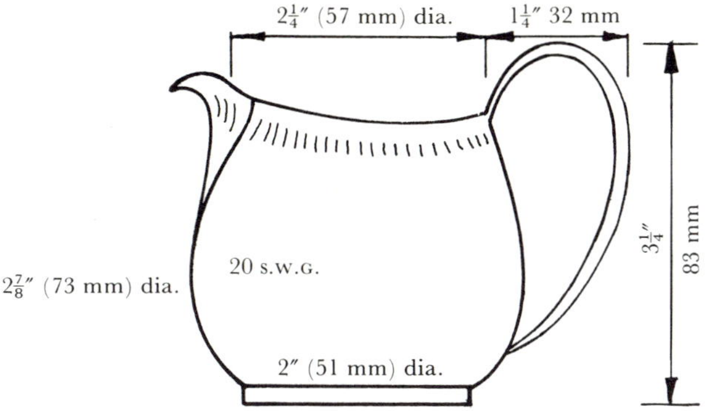

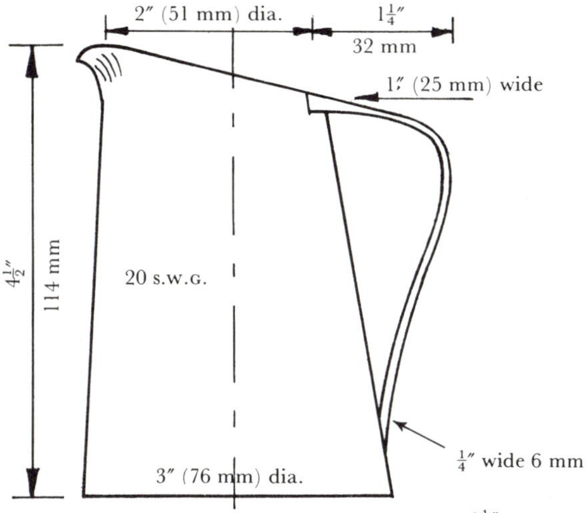

$2\frac{7}{8}''$ (73 mm) dia.

20 s.w.g.

$3\frac{1}{4}''$ 83 mm

2″ (51 mm) dia.

2″ (51 mm) dia. $1\frac{1}{4}''$ 32 mm

1″ (25 mm) wide

$4\frac{1}{2}''$ 114 mm

20 s.w.g.

$\frac{1}{4}''$ wide 6 mm

3″ (76 mm) dia.

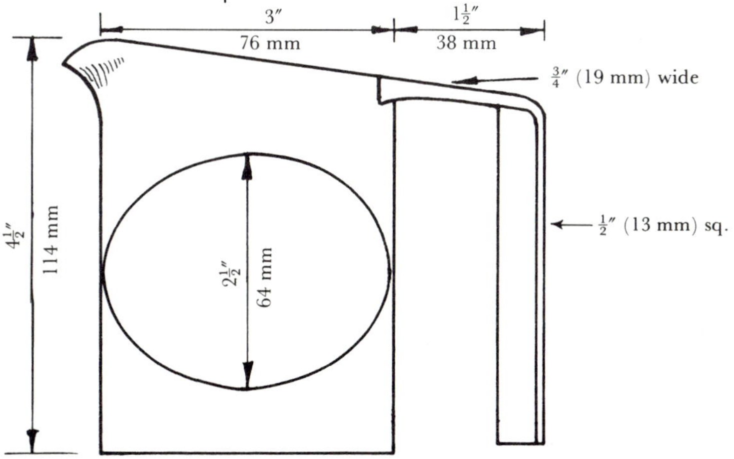

3″ 76 mm $1\frac{1}{2}''$ 38 mm

$\frac{3}{4}''$ (19 mm) wide

$4\frac{1}{2}''$ 114 mm

$2\frac{1}{2}''$ 64 mm

$\frac{1}{2}''$ (13 mm) sq.

TINPLATE MODELS

1 pint or $\frac{1}{2}$ pint capacity? (Or litres?)

Does it pour milk efficiently?

Can the handle be held firmly and comfortably?

Can a handle be dispensed with?

Milk jug

The shape has been adopted after careful observation of milk pouring. This form directs the liquid towards the spout and the widening of the jug from the base maintains an even flow as it is tilted.

Sugar bowl

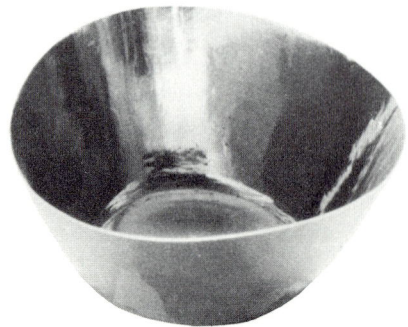

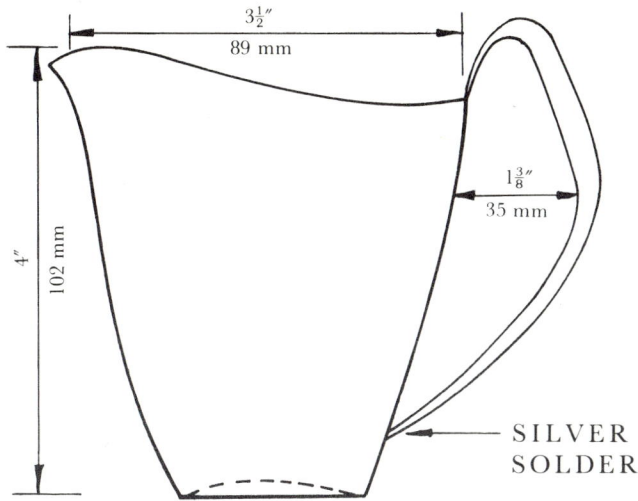

SILVER
SOLDER

RAISING IS STARTED $\frac{3}{4}''$
(19 MM) OFF CENTRE ON A
7″ (178 MM) DISC—18 S.W.G.

The basic techniques of silversmithing are clearly explained and illustrated in the book 'Metalwork and its decoration by Etching' —Author O. Almeida
For silverplating see the address on page 116

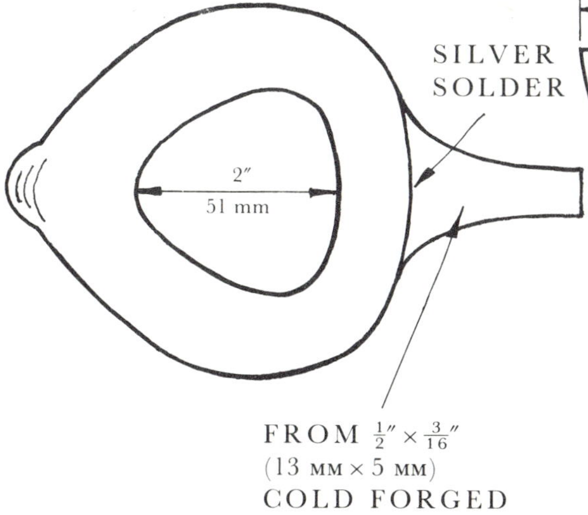

SILVER
SOLDER

2″
51 mm

5″
127 mm

2″
51 mm

FROM $\frac{1}{2}'' \times \frac{3}{16}''$
(13 MM × 5 MM)
COLD FORGED

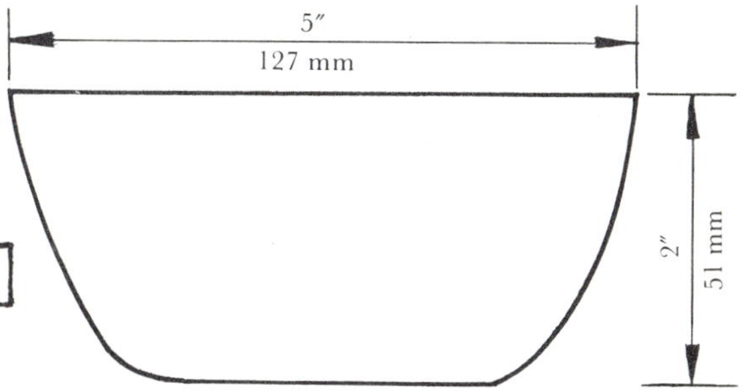

RAISED FROM 7″ (178 MM) DIA × 18 S.W.G.

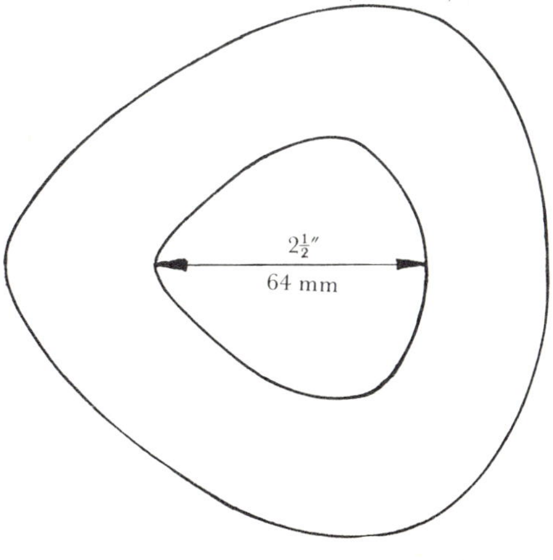

$2\frac{1}{2}''$
64 mm

Milk jug   Sugar bowl   49

Coffee pot

In the initial design stages a number of sketches showing the composition of the coffee pot from several angles is necessary. Can these shapes be formed on the available stakes?

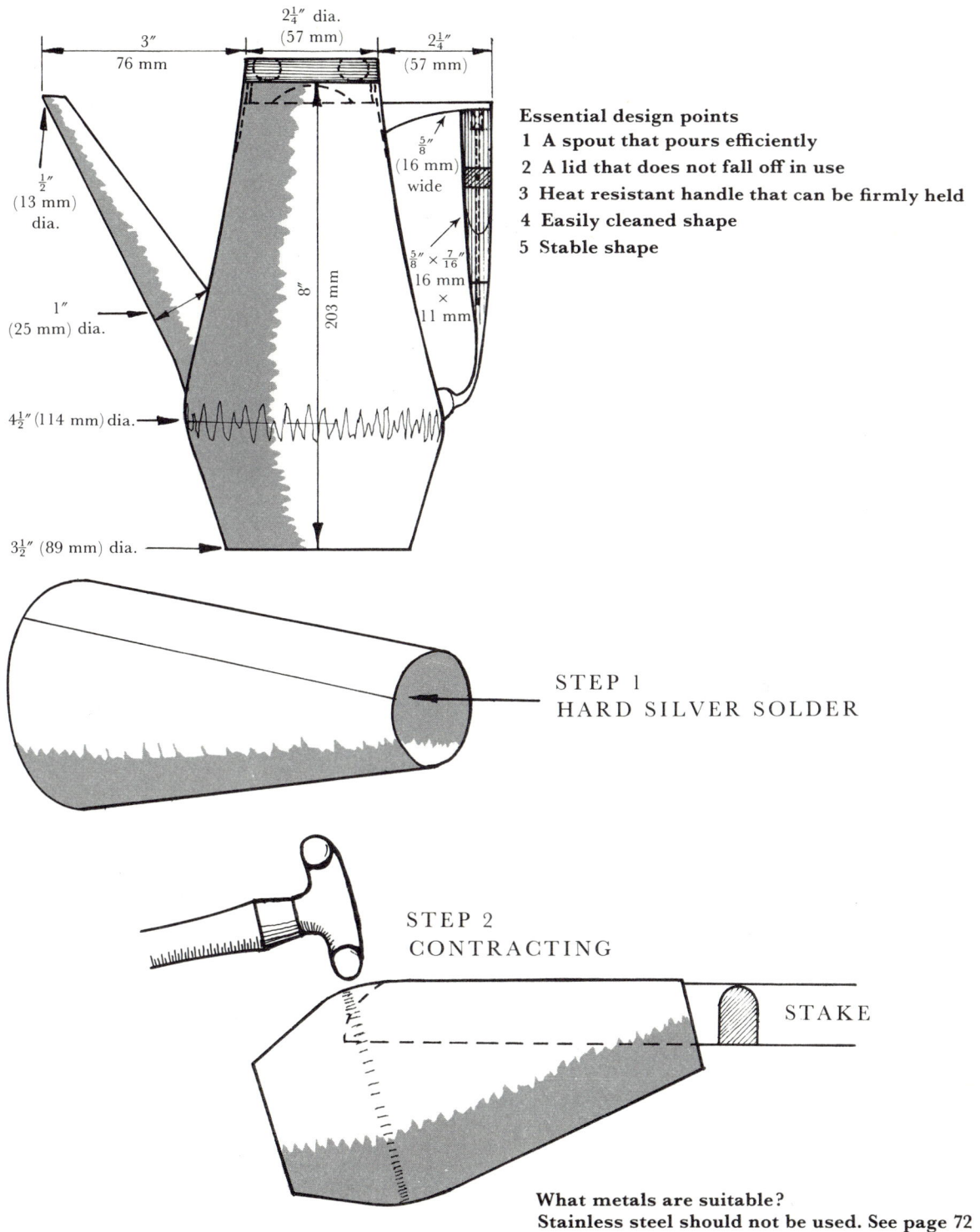

$2\frac{1}{4}''$ dia.
(57 mm)

3″
76 mm

$2\frac{1}{4}''$
(57 mm)

$\frac{1}{2}''$
(13 mm)
dia.

$\frac{5}{8}''$
(16 mm)
wide

1″
(25 mm) dia.

$\frac{5}{8}'' \times \frac{7}{16}''$
16 mm
×
11 mm

8″
203 mm

$4\frac{1}{2}''$ (114 mm) dia.

$3\frac{1}{2}''$ (89 mm) dia.

Essential design points
1 **A spout that pours efficiently**
2 **A lid that does not fall off in use**
3 **Heat resistant handle that can be firmly held**
4 **Easily cleaned shape**
5 **Stable shape**

STEP 1
HARD SILVER SOLDER

STEP 2
CONTRACTING

STAKE

What metals are suitable?
Stainless steel should not be used. See page 72

Salt and pepper set

The method of mounting shown on the drawing, used to ensure accurate centring, requires tops to be fitted after drilling. Metal is used for these tops because it is easy to shape and fit.

With a close grained hardwood like walnut a smooth interior to the pots can be achieved. Flat and domed tops assist in the pouring of the pepper and salt, and make the pots quickly identifiable.

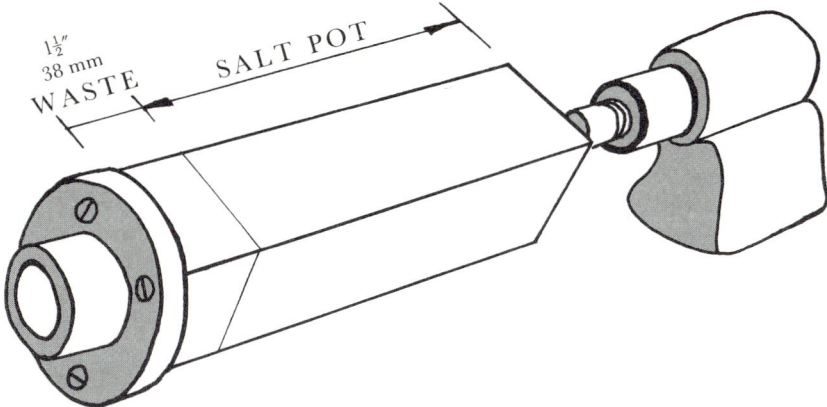

A $2\frac{1}{4}''$ (57 mm) sq. section block can be mounted on a 3″ faceplate. Drive 1″ × No. 10 steel screws in on the diagonals of the block. The end of the block must be perfectly square.

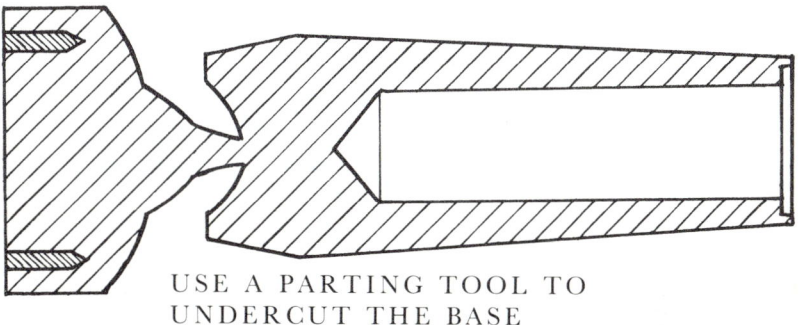

USE A PARTING TOOL TO
UNDERCUT THE BASE

The hole can be drilled out with a morse taper shank drill, set in the tailstock. It can be enlarged if necessary with the edge of a skew chisel

Salt and pepper set

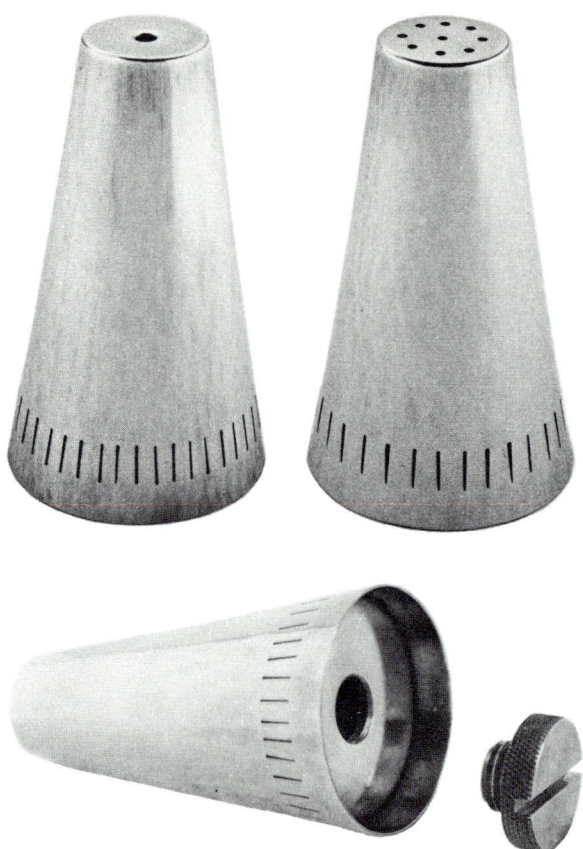

The band of punch work is added to give further interest. If it is to be used this must be decided before commencing work, as it is done at an early stage in the construction.

The metal stopper has a knurled edge and coin slot. Plastic, rubber or cork stoppers could be used and this would simplify the base.

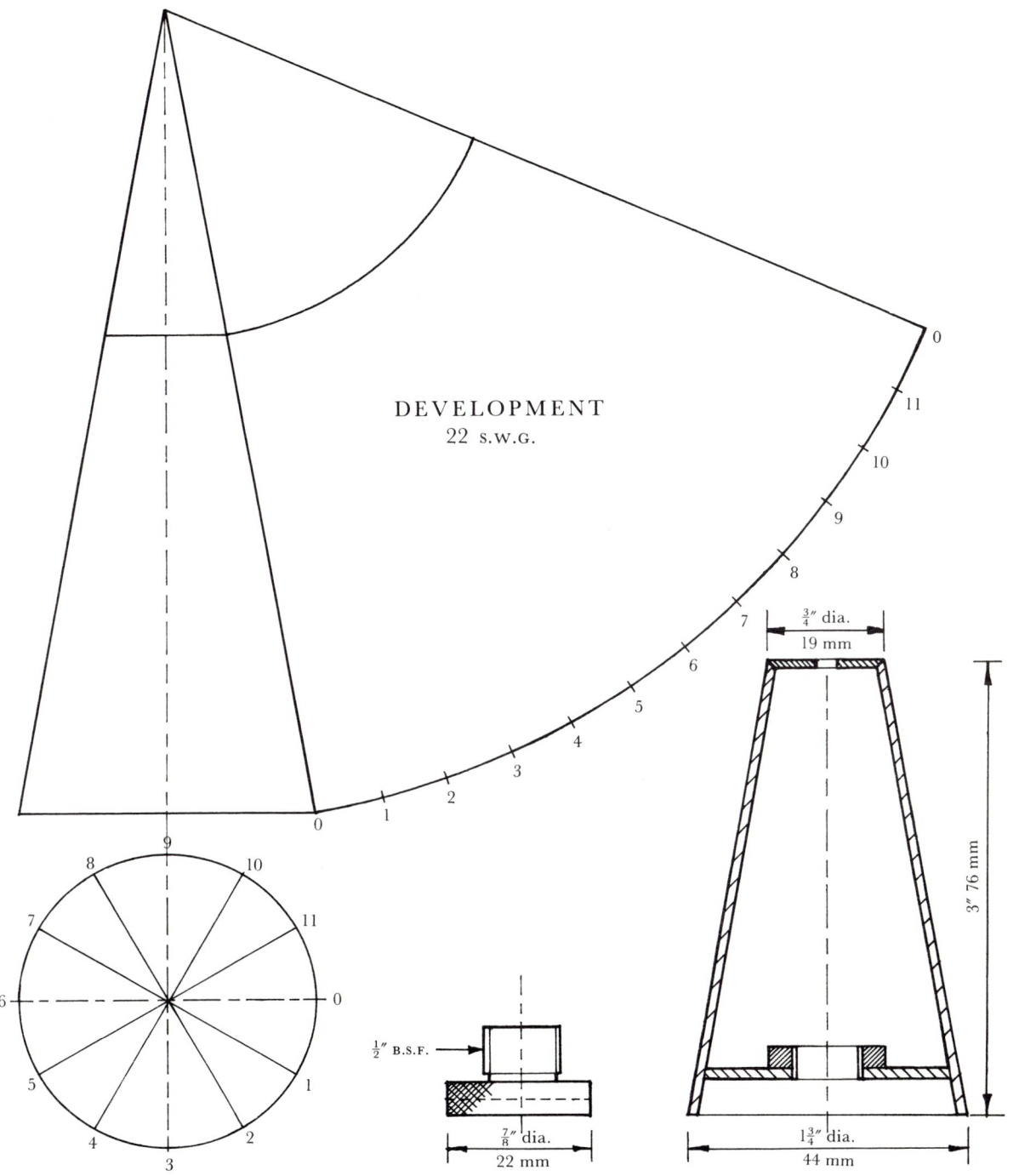

DEVELOPMENT
22 s.w.g.

$\frac{3}{4}''$ dia.
19 mm

$\frac{7}{8}''$ dia.
22 mm

$\frac{1}{2}''$ B.S.F.

3" 76 mm

$1\frac{3}{4}''$ dia.
44 mm

ALL JOINTS SILVER SOLDERED

Cruet set

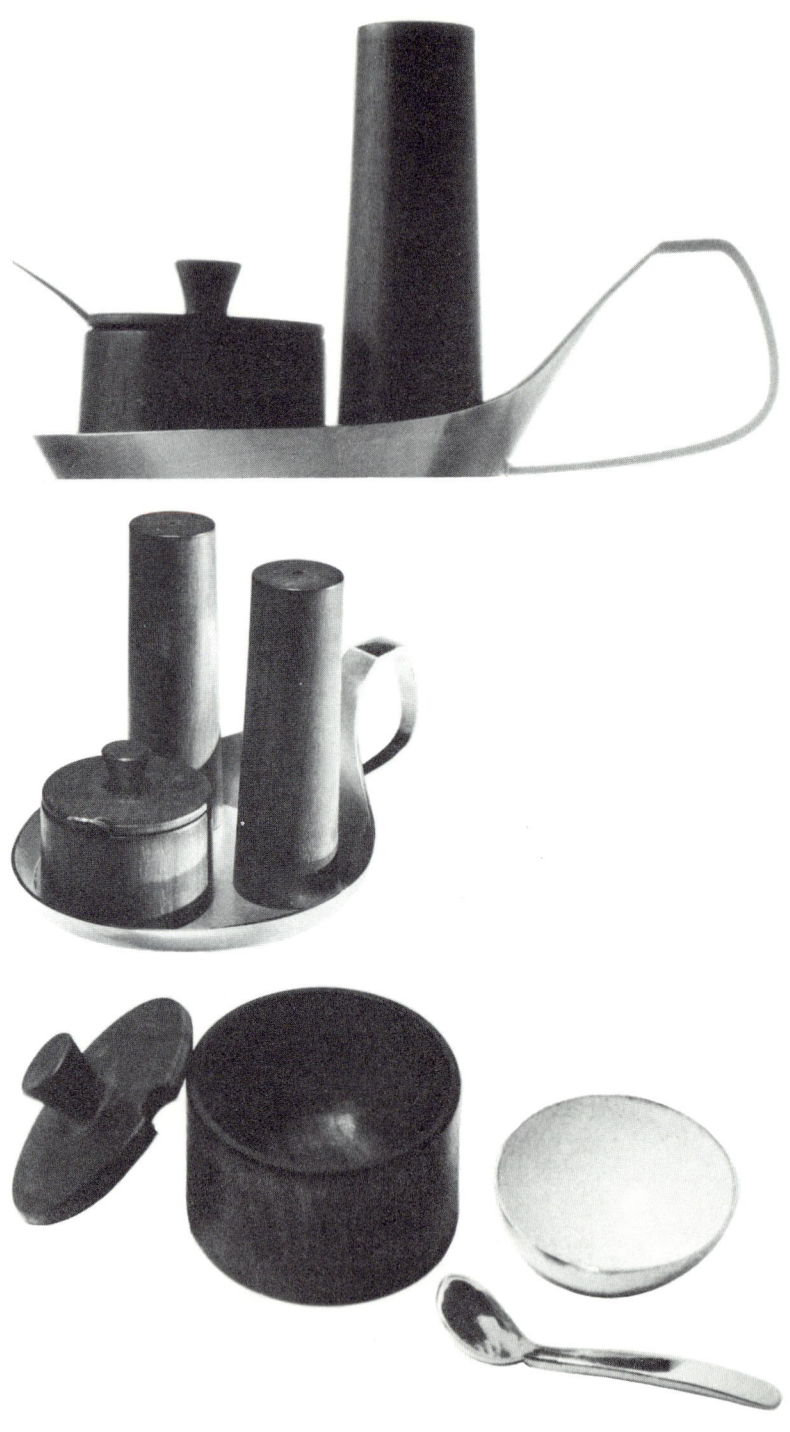

To prevent any reaction with mustard the inside of the pot is enamelled and the spoon is gilt-plated.

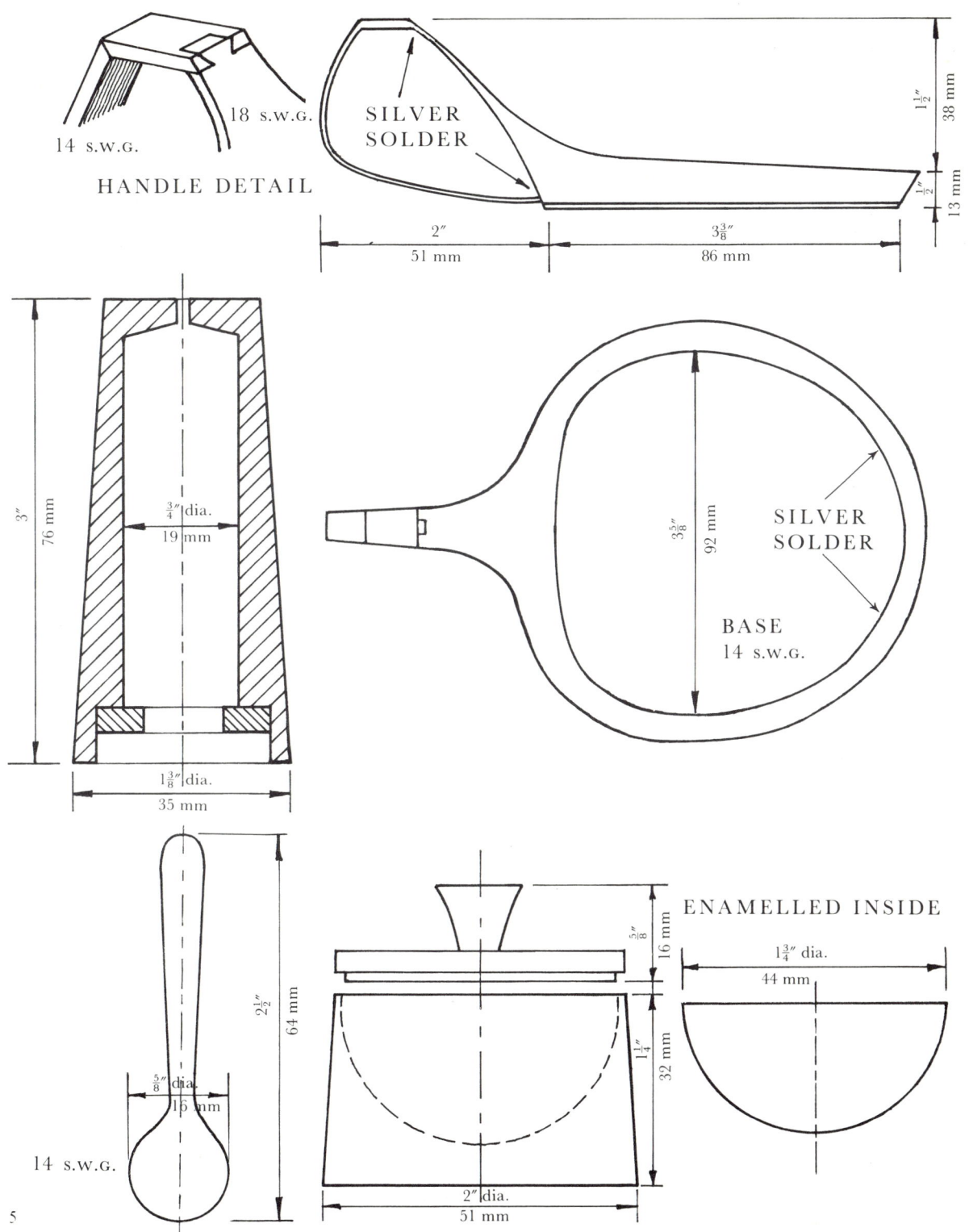

HANDLE DETAIL

14 s.w.g.

18 s.w.g.

SILVER SOLDER

$1\frac{1}{2}''$
38 mm

$\frac{1}{2}''$
13 mm

2"
51 mm

$3\frac{3}{8}''$
86 mm

3"
76 mm

$\frac{3}{4}''$ dia.
19 mm

$1\frac{3}{8}''$ dia.
35 mm

$3\frac{5}{8}''$
92 mm

SILVER SOLDER

BASE
14 s.w.g.

$2\frac{1}{2}''$
64 mm

$\frac{5}{8}''$ dia.
16 mm

14 s.w.g.

$\frac{5}{8}''$
16 mm

$1\frac{1}{4}''$
32 mm

2" dia.
51 mm

ENAMELLED INSIDE

$1\frac{3}{4}''$ dia.
44 mm

5

Cruet set

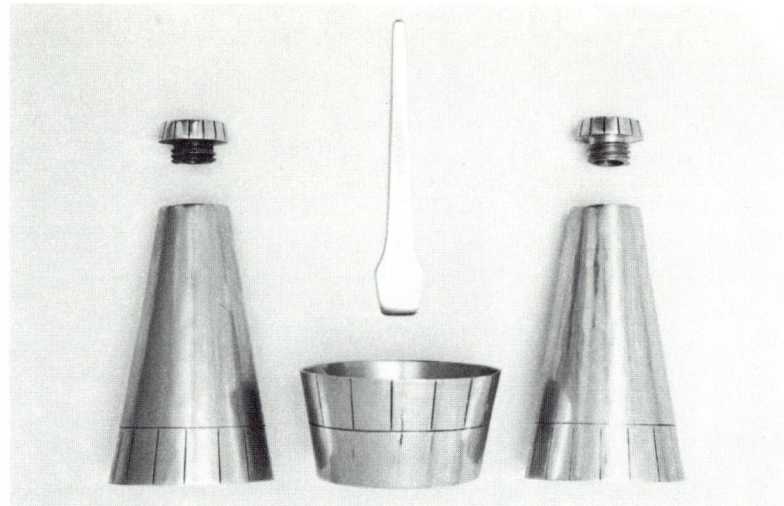

With this set it was decided that the top was the most convenient end for filling salt and pepper pots.

The conical shape was chosen because of its stability, and the edge decoration at the top to give a knurled finger grip. The matching lower band of decoration, the positioning and proportions of which were carefully considered in relation to that at the top, relieves the plain surface and emphasises the outside shape.

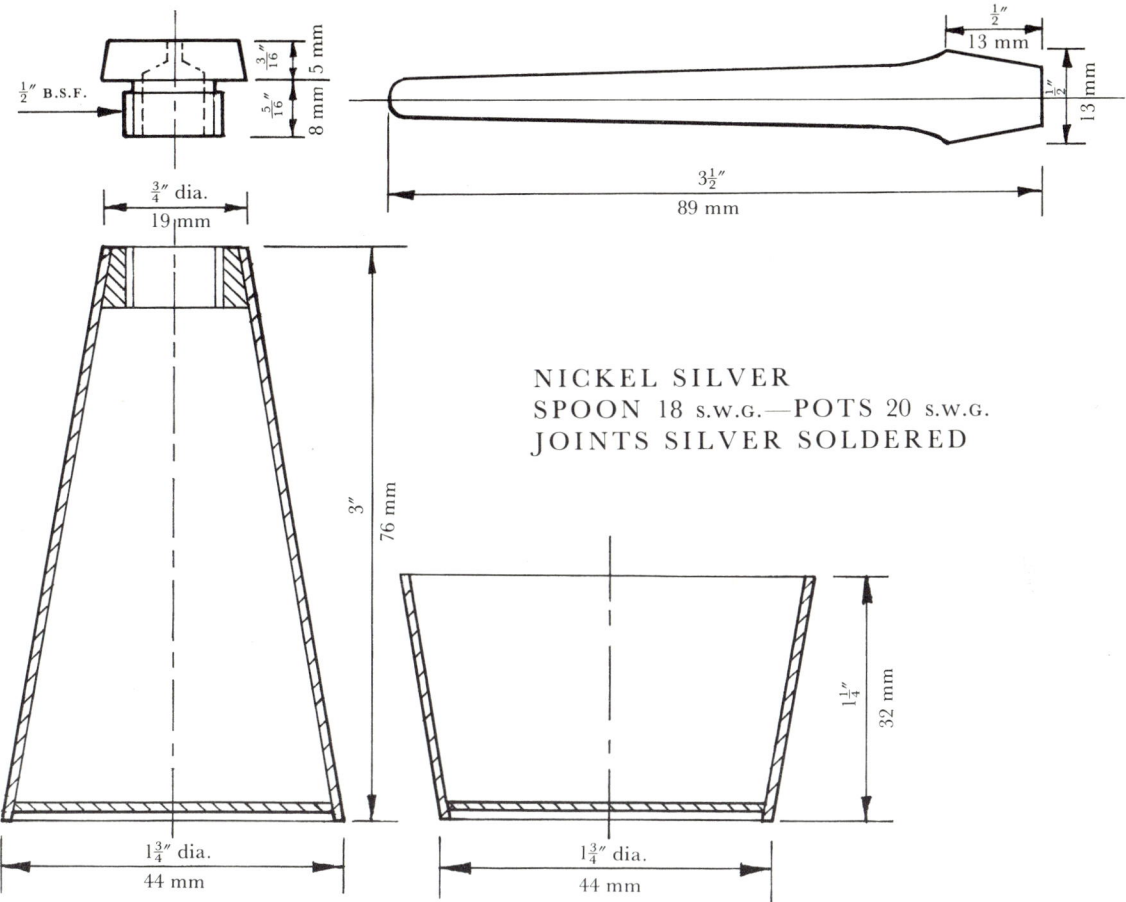

NICKEL SILVER
SPOON 18 s.w.g.—POTS 20 s.w.g.
JOINTS SILVER SOLDERED

Does the mustard pot need a glass lining?

Does the pepper pot need to be as large as the salt pot?

Material—Plated gilding metal? Nickel silver?
Is silver too expensive? Wood and metal?

Is a stand required?

Fruit bowls

You may have a shape in mind for your piece, but here design is very much involved with the material. Faults in the timber can be removed in turning, sapwood turned away on the under edge, cracks or split knots cut out from the hollow side. You must alter the shape to suit the grain and character of the wood. A bowl made from chestnut must surely not be the same thickness or shape as one made from walnut.

Wood is a beautiful material. To cut a clean shape with a sharp gouge and see the grain pattern change as he alters the line will provide a craftsman with far more pleasure than cutting frilly mouldings. Keep the shape simple and functional—the wood should be the attraction not intricate details.

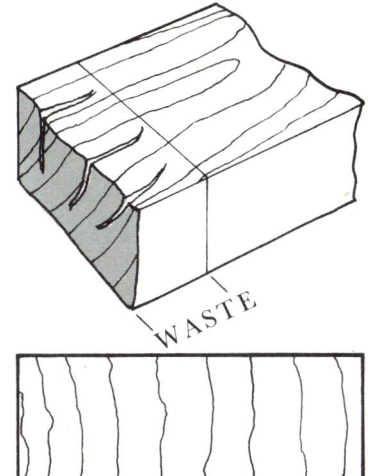

WASTE

End grain cracks where the timber has been exposed to the weather.

Timber cut this way, quarter sawn, is less likely to shrink or warp.

TIMBER FOR
TURNERY

It is difficult to obtain timber of suitable size, well seasoned, fault free, and with an attractive grain the requisites of a good turnery timber. If there is a local timber yard where you can select, some points to bear in mind are:

1 The wood is likely to crack if it is sawn from the end of a new plank, better a piece that has recently been cut, and you can see the end grain.

2 Look for quarter sawn timber, the annual rings should be vertical and fairly even.

3 Look for surface cracks on the face of the plank. They often go deep.

4 When you get a piece home, store it for a month before turning to allow the wood to adjust to the new humidity and temperature conditions.

5 If when you start to turn the wood it appears damp, leave the bowl about $1\frac{1}{4}''$ thick all round, then cover the end grain with beeswax polish and leave to dry out again.

Fruit bowls

When using richly grained timbers such as English Walnut, much of the beauty of the wood would be destroyed if decoration were attempted.

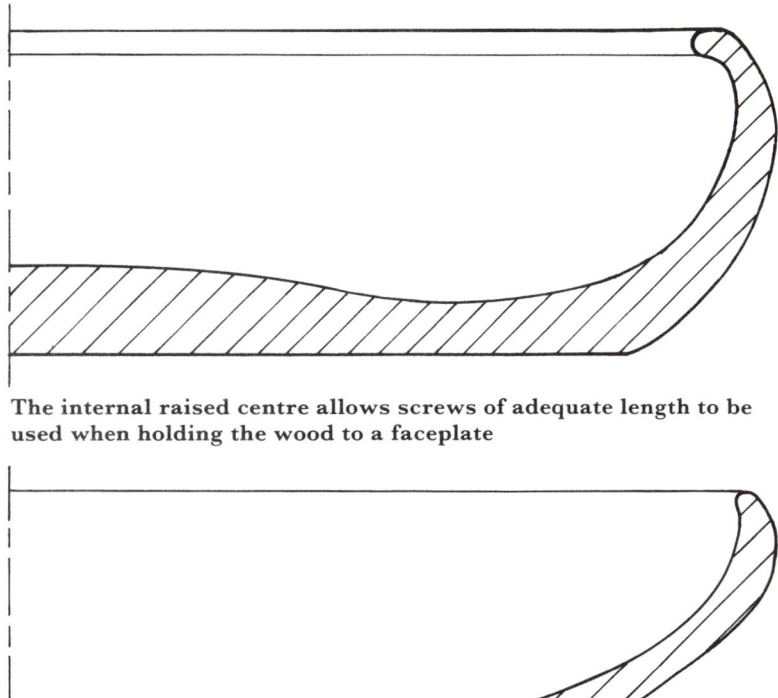

The internal raised centre allows screws of adequate length to be used when holding the wood to a faceplate

The method used in making this bowl involves turning the base of the bowl first, then setting a faceplate in and reversing the bowl. When completed the recess is filled with compressed cork sheet.

Table lamps

A table lamp is a unit formed of base and shade. One cannot be made without reference to the other.

The shade and bulb control the quality of the light, the base puts that light at a suitable height and in doing so must make the whole lamp stable. Like a double-deck bus a lamp must have a low centre of gravity.

Ideas for the lamp base can be sketched full size. These can then be compared with a series of card silhouettes of shades (or their wire frames) available in the local shops.

Clocks

The wall clock transistor movement, obtainable from a jeweller, is operated by a battery having a life of approximately eighteen months.

The movement of the free standing clock was rescued from a discarded case. Is the primary function of a clock fulfilled in these models?

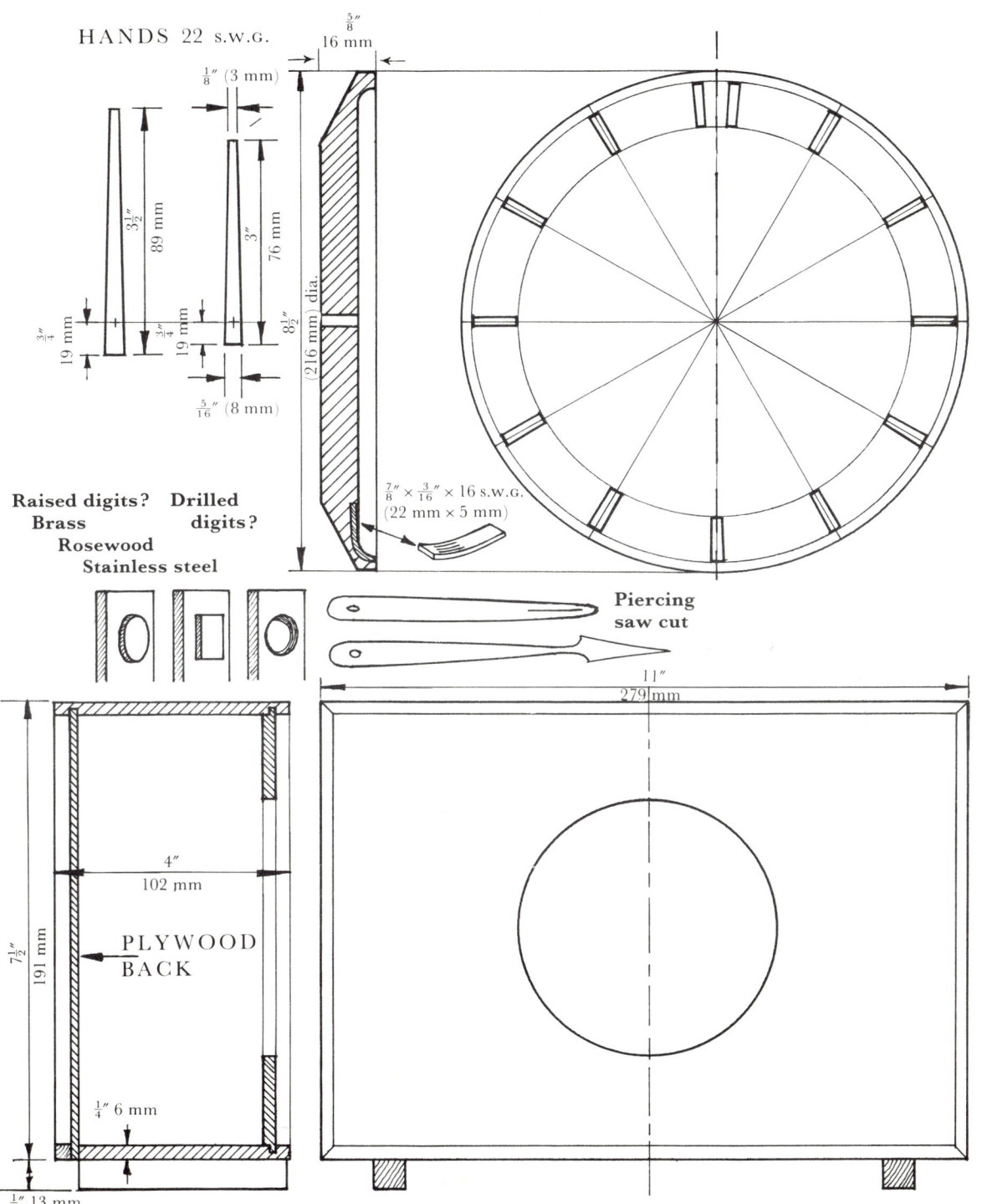

HANDS 22 s.w.g.

$\frac{1}{8}''$ (3 mm)

$\frac{5}{8}''$
16 mm

$3\frac{1}{2}''$
89 mm

$3''$
76 mm

$\frac{3}{4}''$
19 mm

$\frac{3}{4}''$
19 mm

$8\frac{1}{2}''$
(216 mm) dia.

$\frac{5}{16}''$ (8 mm)

Raised digits?
Brass
Rosewood
Stainless steel

Drilled
digits?

$\frac{7}{8}'' \times \frac{3}{16}'' \times 16$ s.w.g.
(22 mm × 5 mm)

Piercing
saw cut

$11''$
279 mm

$4''$
102 mm

PLYWOOD
BACK

$7\frac{1}{2}''$
191 mm

$\frac{1}{4}''$ 6 mm

$\frac{1}{2}''$ 13 mm

Clocks 67

Cotton box

There are practical reasons for the shaping of the box:
1 To lighten the external appearance the wood is shaped away at the base.

2 To give more height for needles and to lighten the lid the underside is concaved.

3 To allow the cotton colours to be freely seen the pin cushion is lowered and the base inside is sloped.

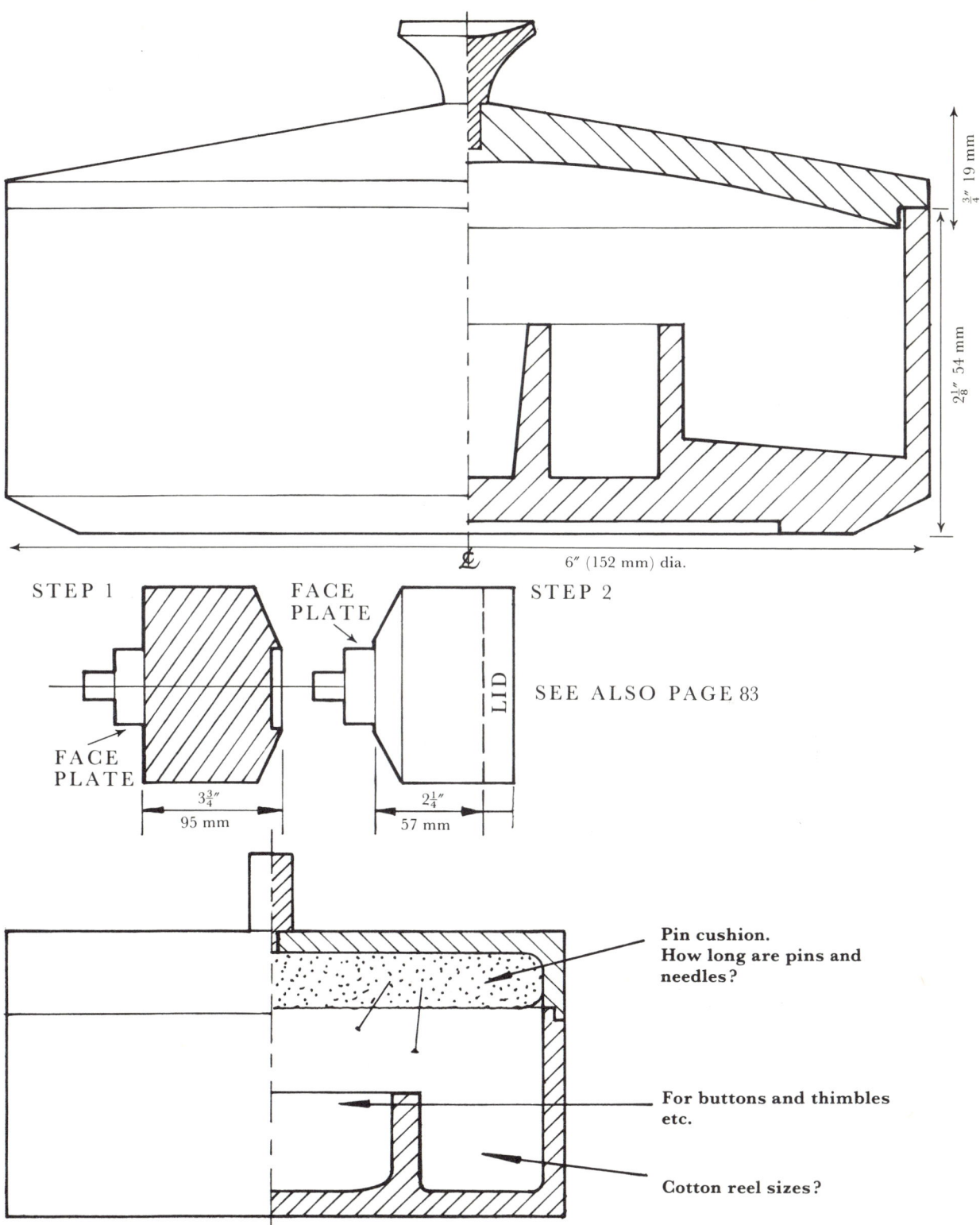

$\frac{3}{4}''$ 19 mm

$2\frac{1}{8}''$ 54 mm

6″ (152 mm) dia.

STEP 1

FACE
PLATE

FACE
PLATE

STEP 2

LID

SEE ALSO PAGE 83

$3\frac{3}{4}''$
95 mm

$2\frac{1}{4}''$
57 mm

Pin cushion.
How long are pins and
needles?

For buttons and thimbles
etc.

Cotton reel sizes?

Cotton box 69

Work box

Accessibility to the box and drawer from an easy chair was a consideration when deciding the height of the stand.
Lapped dovetails are used because grooves locate the box top and bottom, and staggered shelf rails simplify the construction of the underframing.
Stops at the back of the drawer prevent its unintentional removal.
The underside of the box lid is padded to make a pincushion.

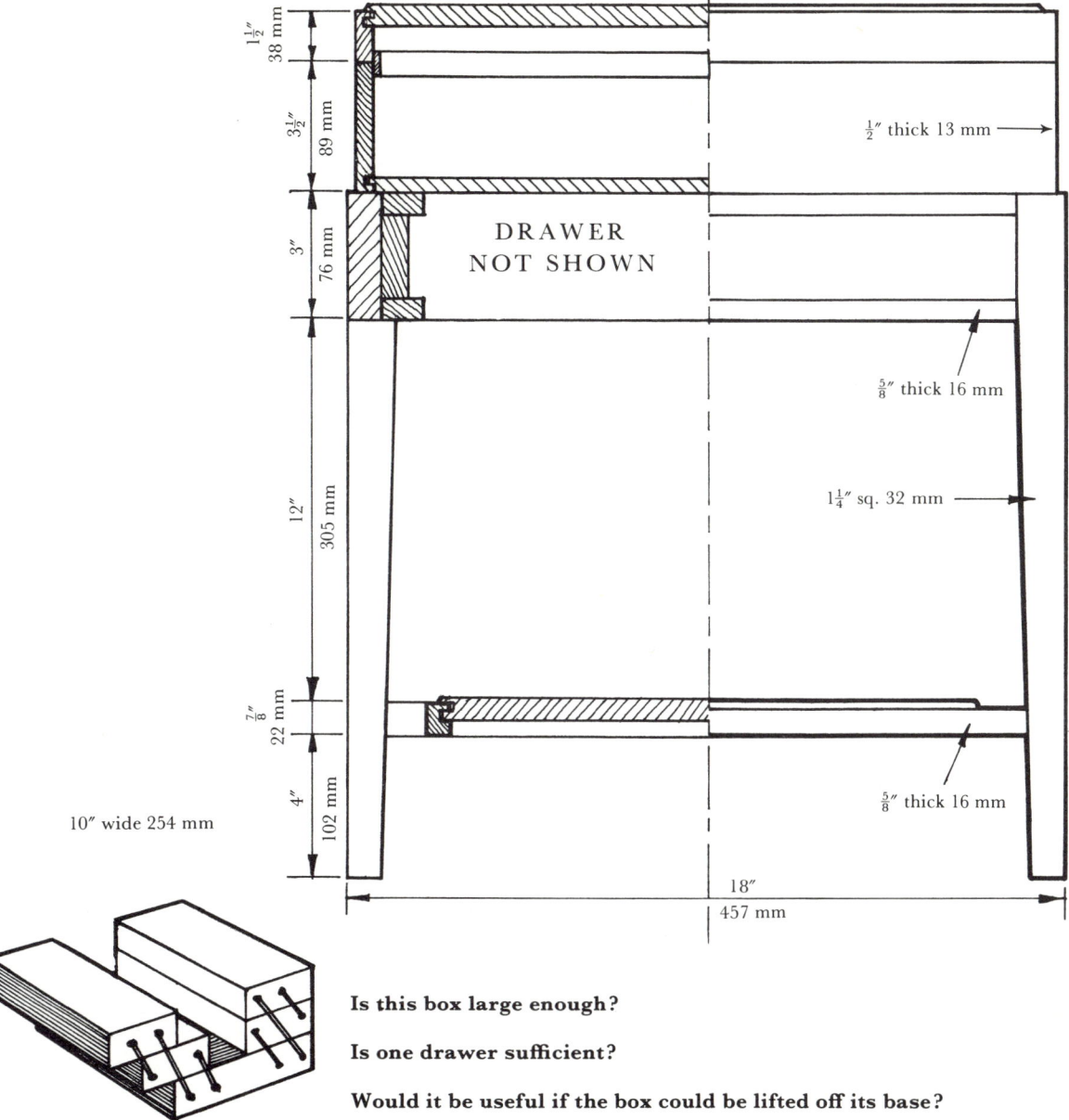

$1\frac{1}{2}''$ 38 mm

$3\frac{1}{2}''$ 89 mm

$\frac{1}{2}''$ thick 13 mm →

3" 76 mm

DRAWER
NOT SHOWN

$\frac{5}{8}''$ thick 16 mm

12" 305 mm

$1\frac{1}{4}''$ sq. 32 mm →

$\frac{7}{8}''$ 22 mm

4" 102 mm

$\frac{5}{8}''$ thick 16 mm

10" wide 254 mm

18"
457 mm

Is this box large enough?

Is one drawer sufficient?

Would it be useful if the box could be lifted off its base?

Money box

When heated, stainless steel produces an extremely hard oxide that is difficult to remove, so its use calls for simplicity of construction and shape, as is illustrated in this money box. The rosewood and stainless steel are joined with a resin adhesive, and together these materials make a pleasing contrast.

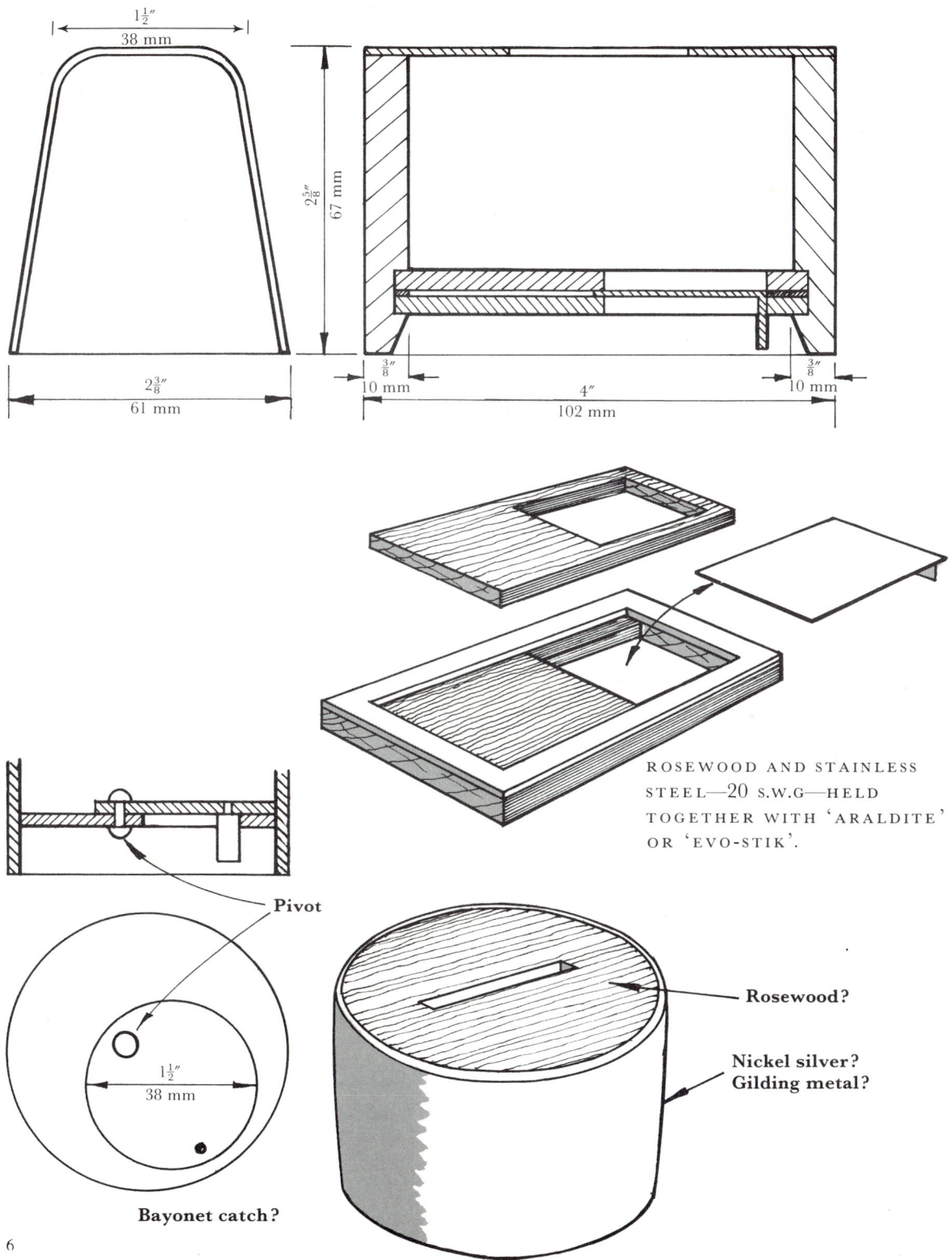

1½″
38 mm

2⅝″
67 mm

2⅜″
61 mm

⅜″
10 mm

4″
102 mm

⅜″
10 mm

ROSEWOOD AND STAINLESS
STEEL—20 S.W.G—HELD
TOGETHER WITH 'ARALDITE'
OR 'EVO-STIK'.

Pivot

1½″
38 mm

Bayonet catch?

Rosewood?

Nickel silver?
Gilding metal?

6

Domino set

These dominoes are made by glueing a length of plastic laminate to wood, then sawn into pieces. The dots are made by drilling and the centre line by sawing through the top layer of laminate, thus exposing the brown core. Choose a piece of wood with an even grain line otherwise the dominoes can be identified from the reverse side. The plastic can, of course, be glued to both sides.

An alternative domino is shown in the photographs. Brass rod is set in to form the spots, and a rosewood strip the dividing line.

SECTIONAL FRONT VIEW

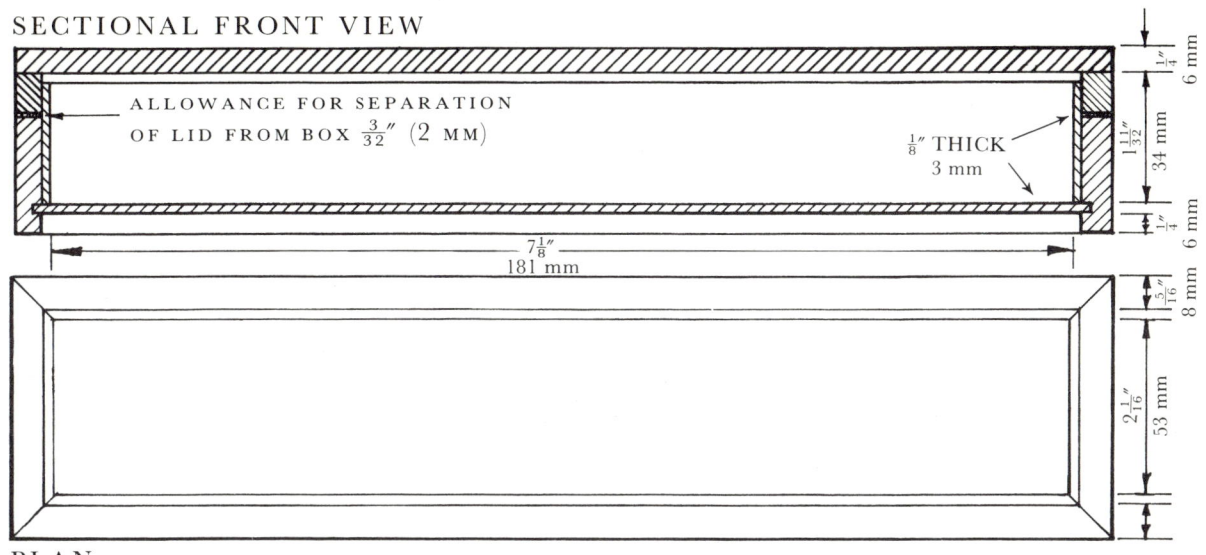

ALLOWANCE FOR SEPARATION
OF LID FROM BOX $\frac{3}{32}''$ (2 MM)

$\frac{1}{8}''$ THICK
3 mm

$\frac{1}{4}''$ 6 mm

$1\frac{11}{32}''$ 34 mm

$\frac{1}{4}''$ 6 mm

$7\frac{1}{8}''$
181 mm

$\frac{5}{16}''$ 8 mm

$2\frac{1}{16}''$ 53 mm

PLAN

The best method of designing this type of box is to draw the plan view of the space needed and work outwards.

Project the front view from the plan.

How much space is needed?

Dominoes in this set are $2'' \times 1'' \times \frac{5}{16}''$ (51 mm × 25 mm × 8 mm).

7 piles of 4 + clearance = $7\frac{1}{8}'' \times 2\frac{1}{16}'' \times 1\frac{1}{4}''$ (181 mm × 53 mm × 32 mm).

THE BOX IS MADE UP AND THE TOP GLUED DOWN WITHOUT THE LININGS. WHEN PLANED PERFECTLY TRUE, THE LID CAN BE SAWN OFF THE BOX. GLUEING THE LID DIRECTLY TO THE BOX IS TECHNICALLY INCORRECT, FOR IF THE TOP SHRINKS IT IS LIKELY TO PULL THE LID OUT OF SHAPE. THIS TENDENCY IS MINIMISED BY USING QUARTER SAWN TIMBER. IN THE CIGARETTE AND JEWELLERY BOXES THE CORRECT METHOD OF ALLOWING FOR SHRINKAGE IS SHOWN.

Suggested joint.

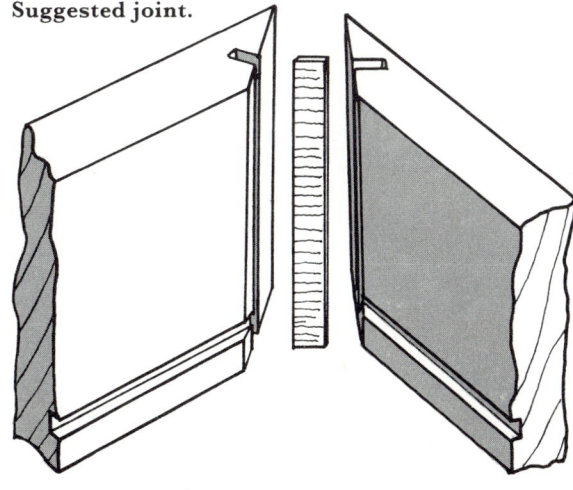

Trinket box

Cigarette box

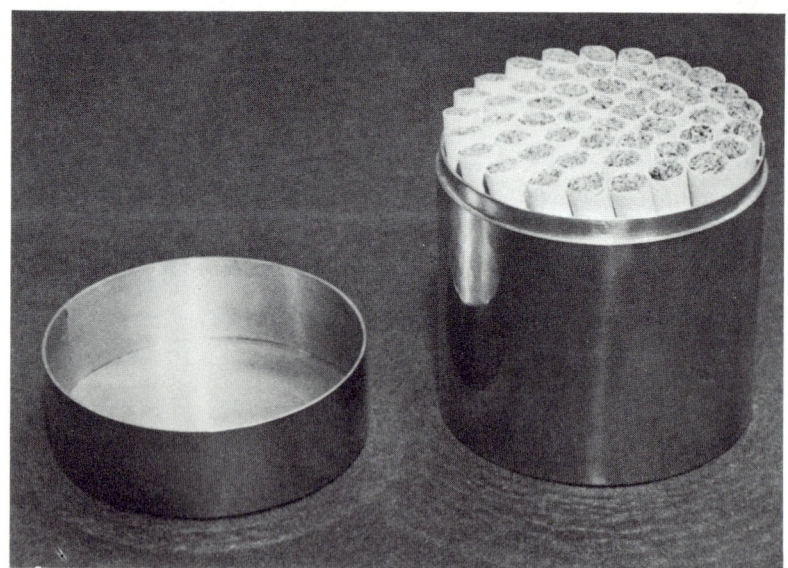

Both boxes are made by forming a cylinder, then cutting through to form lid and box, thus ensuring that they match each other exactly. Whereas the dimensions of the trinket box are not critical, the height and diameter of the cigarette box are dependent upon the type of cigarette to be contained.

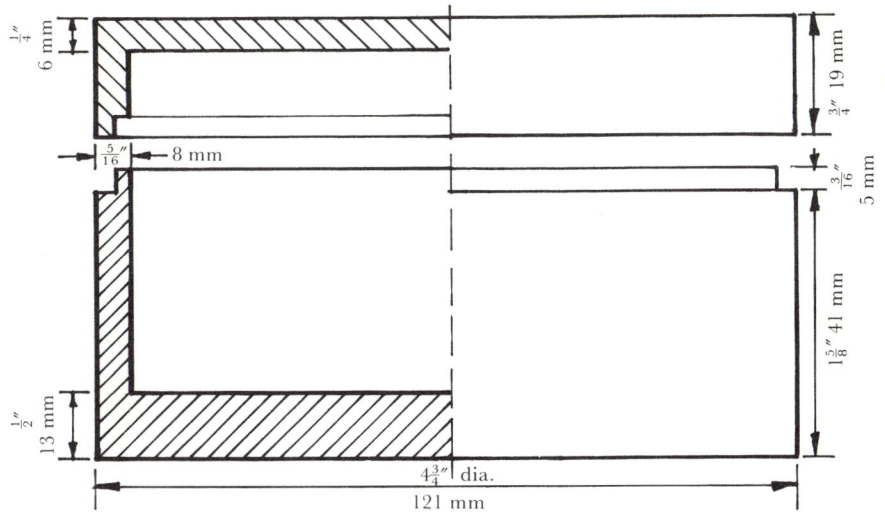

Wood used should be quarter sawn and thoroughly seasoned to minimize shrinkage

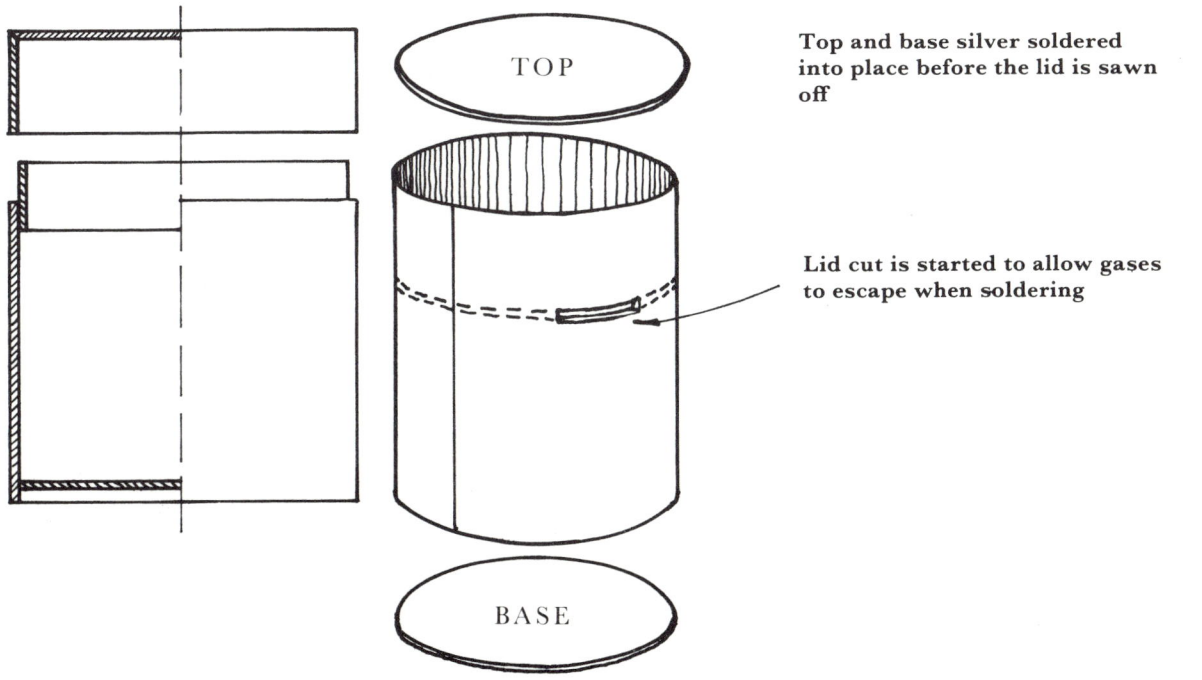

Top and base silver soldered into place before the lid is sawn off

Lid cut is started to allow gases to escape when soldering

Cigarette box

The dimensions of the compartments, and hence the box, are largely dependent upon the capacity required for fifty king size cigarettes. The raised lining aims at providing airtight storage, and the curved fillets allow easier removal of the last few cigarettes. This box is made from Laburnum and has a Mahogany lining.

ALLOW $\frac{3}{32}''$ (2 mm)
TO SAW APART

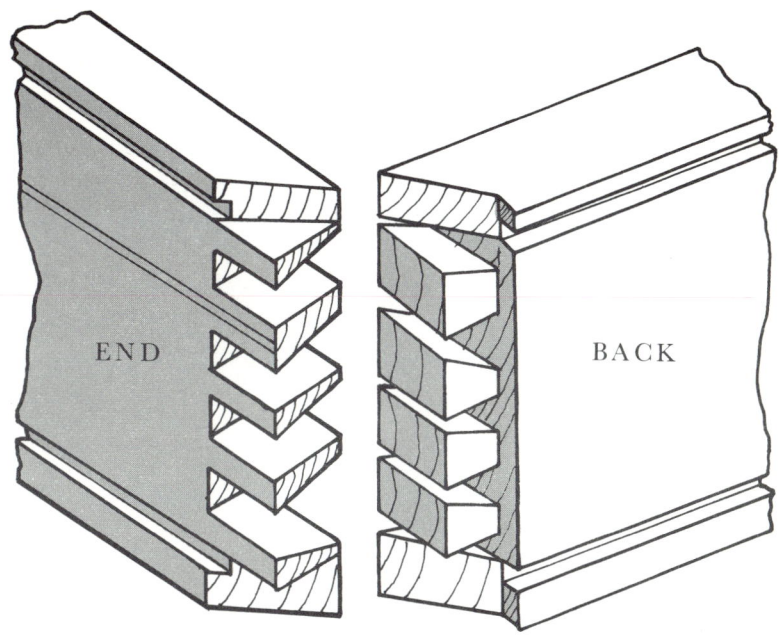

THE SKETCH SHOWS HOW THE EXTRA THICKNESS IN THE
BACK FOR HINGING IS TAKEN UP IN THE JOINT, THUS
LEAVING THE DOVETAILS SHOWING THE SAME THICKNESS
AT THE FRONT AND THE BACK.

END SECTION OF THE BOX

THE TOP IS MADE FROM A WELL GRAINED BLOCK,
QUARTERED AND SET WITHIN A MITRED FRAME. NOTE THE
ALLOWANCE FOR MOVEMENT WITHIN THE GROOVES.

Jewellery box

Like the cigarette box on page 78 this is an article whose demands
upon patience, care and skill will delight a craftsman who is intent
upon producing what is more than a mere utility. English Walnut
and Sycamore have been used for this box.

How big should a jewellery box be? This one is 8″ (203 mm) long by 4″ (102 mm) wide by 2¾″ (70 mm) high, but some ladies have more jewellery than others!

TO MAKE UP THE TOP AN ATTRACTIVELY GRAINED BLOCK IS CAREFULLY PLANED TO SIZE. THEN CUT THE THICKNESS IN HALF WITH A FINE TOOTHED SAW. THE INSIDE FACES WHEN PLANED WILL MATCH.

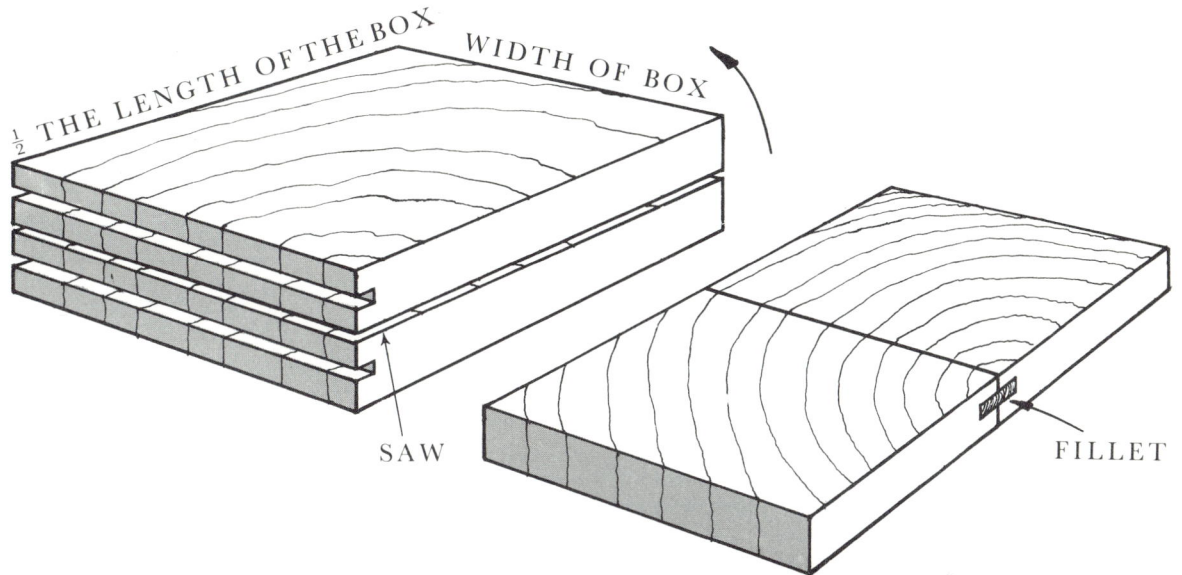

A SMALL FILLET IS GLUED IN A GROOVE TO STRENGTHEN THE END GRAIN JOINT. THE WHOLE TOP IS THEN GROOVED AND REBATED INTO THE BOX, TAKING CARE THAT THE FILLET IS CONCEALED WITHIN THE JOINT.

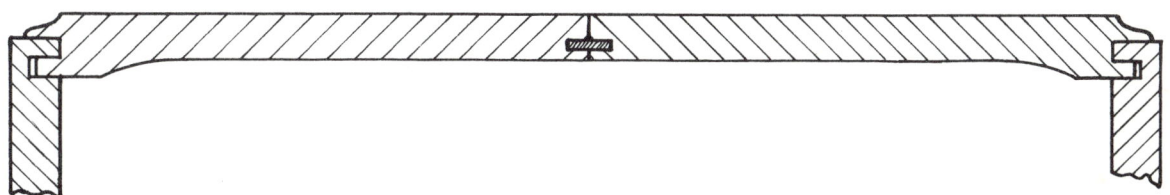

TO REDUCE THE WEIGHT OF THE TOP, THE UNDERNEATH OF THE LID HAS BEEN CARVED AWAY. IN THIS BOX A TEXTURED GOUGE SURFACE HAS BEEN LEFT.

Trinket box

The lid can be removed easily with one hand, so a knob is not necessary.
Decorative qualities arise naturally, the colour, grain and matt finish of the English Walnut contrasting with the planished, polished gilding metal.

BOX JOINTS SOLDERED AS ON PAGE 85

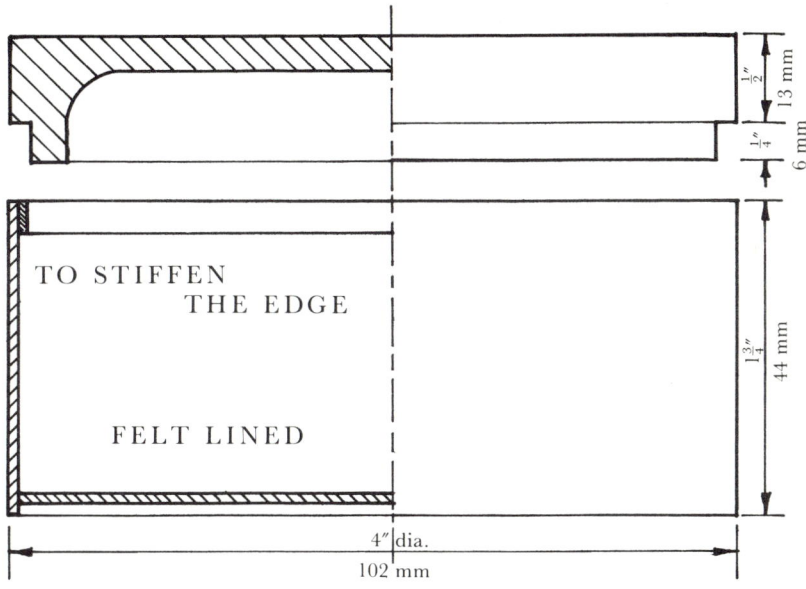

$\frac{1}{2}''$
13 mm

$\frac{1}{4}''$
6 mm

TO STIFFEN
THE EDGE

FELT LINED

$1\frac{3}{4}''$
44 mm

4″ dia.
102 mm

Methods of holding the lid for turning

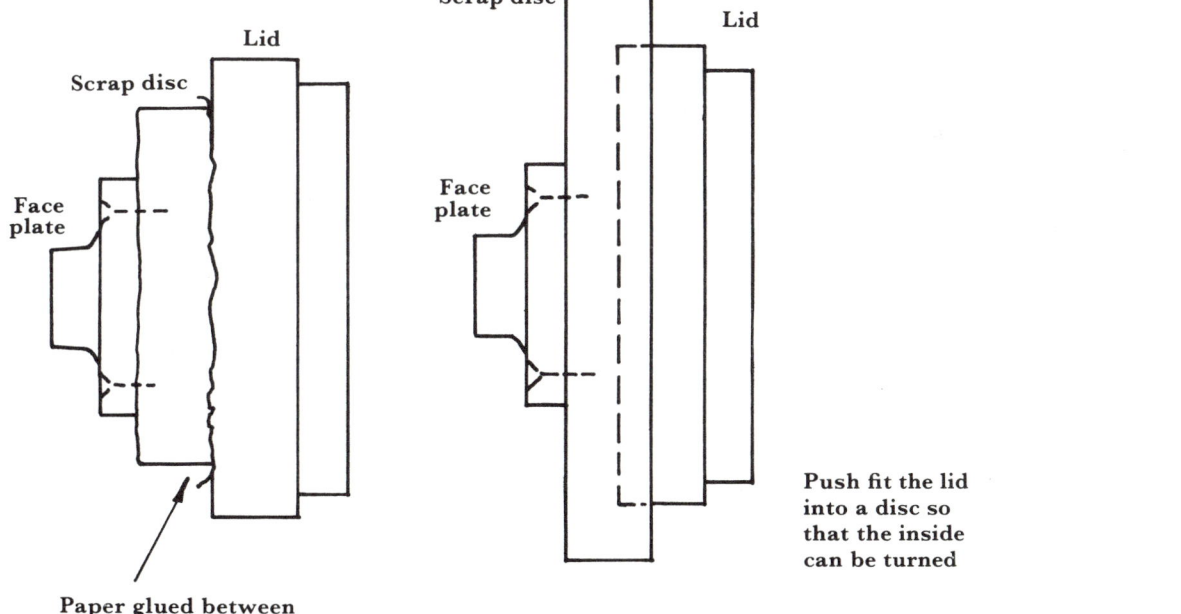

Lid

Scrap disc

Face plate

Paper glued between
the scrap disc and lid

Scrap disc

Lid

Face plate

Push fit the lid
into a disc so
that the inside
can be turned

Trinket box

Proportions are of great importance and can only be clearly assessed using three-dimensional models. In this case full size paper models were critically examined. The result is an economical, straightforward box construction, where the simple outside shape, the knob and decoration are all in harmony.
The colour of the rosewood and the glow from the planished gilding metal add a warmth not apparent in the photograph.

SIDES BUTT JOINTED AND HARD SOLDERED.
OTHER JOINTS EASY FLO SILVER SOLDERED.

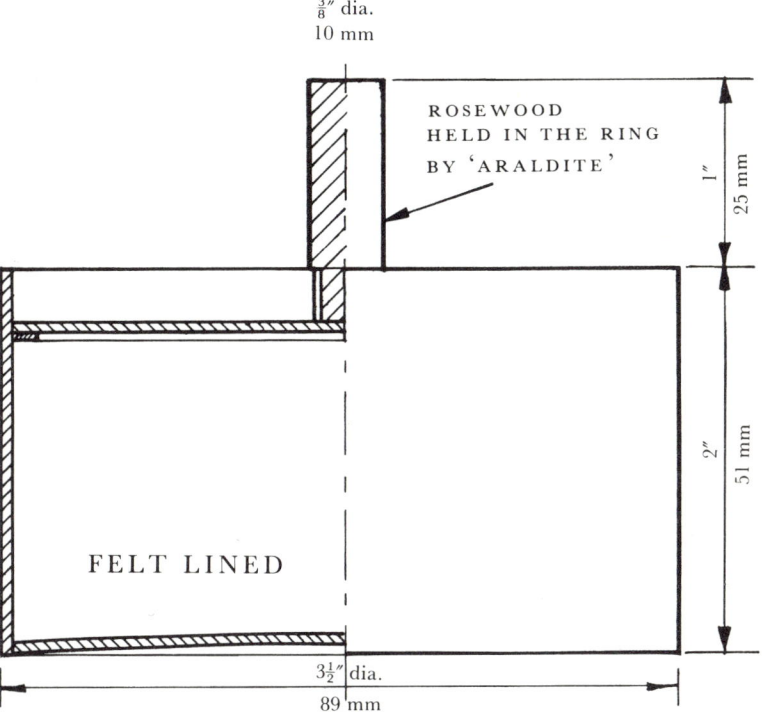

$\frac{3}{8}''$ dia.
10 mm

ROSEWOOD
HELD IN THE RING
BY 'ARALDITE'

1"
25 mm

2"
51 mm

FELT LINED

$3\frac{1}{2}''$ dia.
89 mm

METAL 18 s.w.g.   **Gilding metal? Silverplated? Nickel silver? Silver?**

FINISH   **Highly polished or matt? Protective finish of lacquer or wax that will not require further cleaning?**

Rings and bracelets

The size and shape of these rings and bracelets should be made to fit and suit the wearer.

An effective decoration is the repetition of one simple motif where the plain surfaces also play an important part.

Brooches

The overall shape of the centre of interest in these brooches
controls the shape and form of the mountings and decoration.
Such forms of decoration are present in Nature and Mathematics.
(The two engraved pieces of mother of pearl and Chinese counters
were found in an antique shop.)

Jewellery

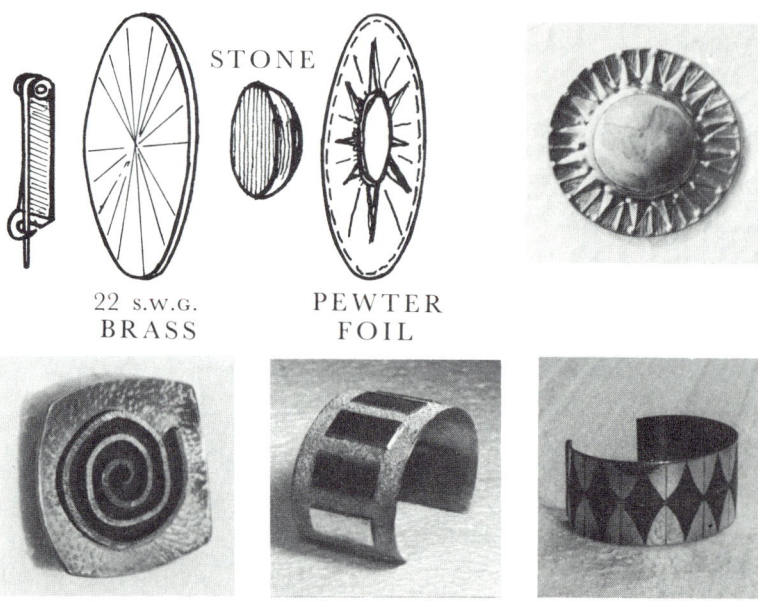

STONE

22 s.w.g.
BRASS

PEWTER
FOIL

The effectiveness of the decoration on these items lies in the contrasts. The smooth surfaces are polished before using a vibrating tool to obtain the roughened texture.

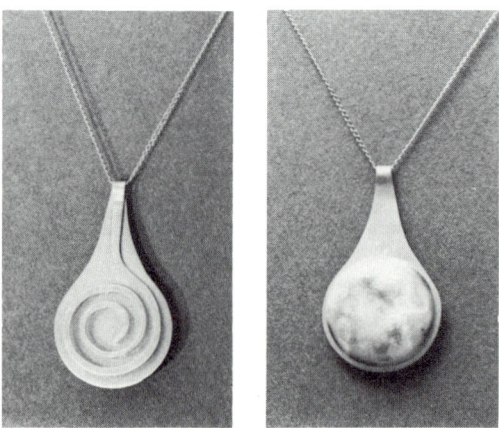

The form of the snail suggested the shape for this pendant which will hang with either face offering an interest.

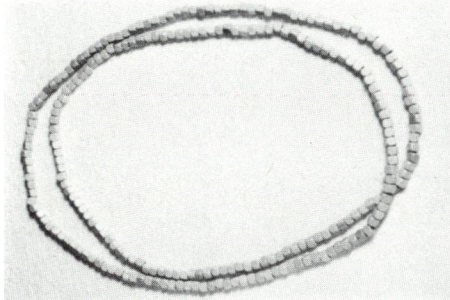

These wooden beads are from Scandinavia. The grain and colour in wood when allied to simple shapes suggest many interesting ideas for jewellery.

A considerable variety of colours and patterns is possible by enamelling simple copper shapes.
A few of the excellent books on the making and designing of jewellery are listed on page 117.

7

Wood carving

Some good books are available on wood carving. It is not the intention to enlarge upon their work but to show how close is the link between material and design.

One approach is to explore the character of the wood, the grain, the knots, by cutting and chiseling, without attempting to impose any preconceived ideas upon the material.

Having some knowledge of the structure of the material we can use this when developing ideas and shapes. Fish, animal and other natural forms provide much inspiration for carving, fish shapes being probably the easiest form to adapt to the material, the grain showing the flow of line and movement.

The grain pattern can also suggest the actual form of the carving.
The fish was carved from a piece of short grain walnut. With the
splits and knots removed the form developed. In the bison the
grain pattern of the Western Hemlock is used to emphasise the
shape and strength of the animal.

Wood carving

For this bird form, an idea was sketched out on a block of walnut, and the bulk of the waste sawn away, but the line, shape and position of neck, head and tail were developed by following the grain pattern and flow of the wood.

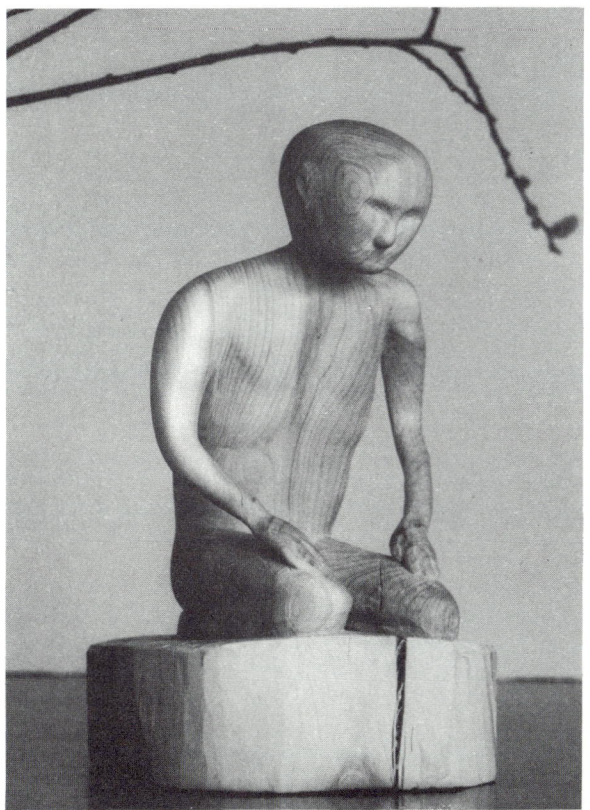

The value to the beginner lies in what is learnt from the study of more complicated forms, rather than in successfully completed carvings. Dealing with a grain pattern so wild as that of the yew in this example, also presents a challenge to the technical skills of the carver.

Letter racks
Paper knife

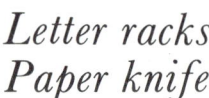

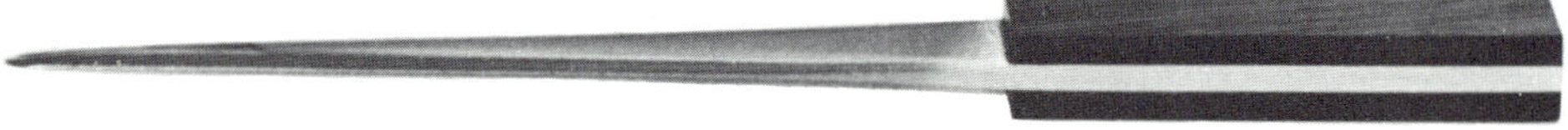

The rectangular shapes of the letter racks follow that of the envelope.
Both racks are of similar construction.
A simple, efficient shape is used for the paper knife, the decorative qualities arising naturally.

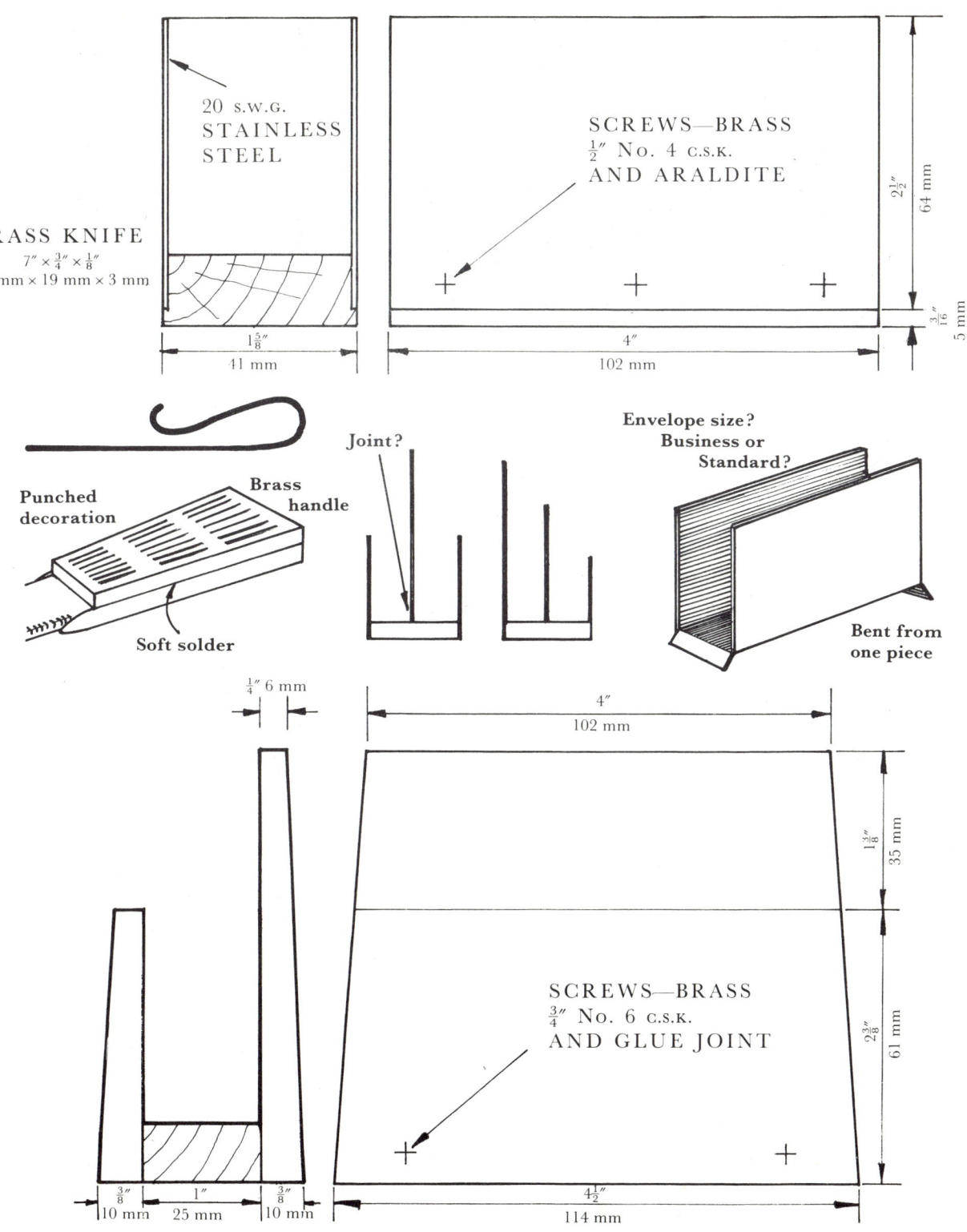

20 s.w.g.
STAINLESS
STEEL

BRASS KNIFE
$7'' \times \frac{3}{4}'' \times \frac{1}{8}''$
8 mm × 19 mm × 3 mm

SCREWS—BRASS
$\frac{1}{2}''$ No. 4 c.s.k.
AND ARALDITE

$2\frac{1}{2}''$ 64 mm

$\frac{3}{16}''$ 5 mm

$1\frac{5}{8}''$ 41 mm

$4''$ 102 mm

Punched decoration

Brass handle

Soft solder

Joint?

Envelope size?
Business or
Standard?

Bent from
one piece

$\frac{1}{4}''$ 6 mm

$4''$ 102 mm

$1\frac{3}{8}''$ 35 mm

SCREWS—BRASS
$\frac{3}{4}''$ No. 6 c.s.k.
AND GLUE JOINT

$2\frac{3}{8}''$ 61 mm

$\frac{3}{8}''$ 10 mm $1''$ 25 mm $\frac{3}{8}''$ 10 mm

$4\frac{1}{2}''$ 114 mm

Small dish

A fluid shape where dish and base are in complete harmony. Made from a design by K. H. Smith, A.T.D. Senior Lecturer, Loughborough College of Art and Design.

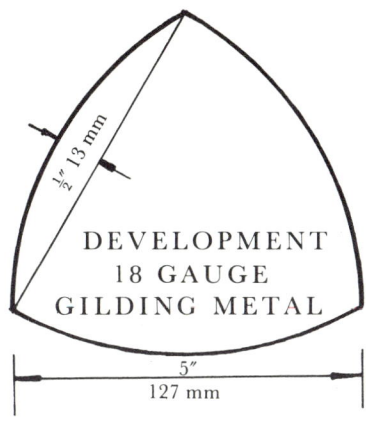

DEVELOPMENT
18 GAUGE
GILDING METAL

½″ 13 mm

5″
127 mm

What do you expect to put in your dish? Or will it be mainly decorative?

Regular shapes are used on the few dishes shown in this book. Consider the possibilities of free shapes.

Aluminium is useful for trying out these dish shapes.

STEP 1

$6\frac{3}{4}″ \times \frac{3}{16}″$ dia.
171 mm × 5 mm

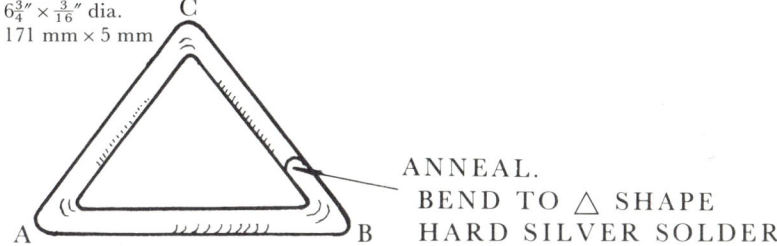

ANNEAL.
BEND TO △ SHAPE
HARD SILVER SOLDER

STEP 2

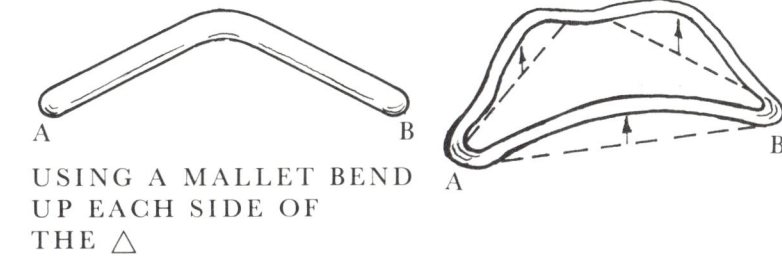

USING A MALLET BEND
UP EACH SIDE OF
THE △

STEP 3   THE BASE FINALLY COMPLETED, TO THE SHAPE SHOWN IN THE PHOTOGRAPHS, BY FLATTENING WITH A PLANISHING HAMMER ON A FLAT STAKE.

USE EASY FLO SILVER SOLDER BETWEEN THE BASE AND DISH.

Dishes

In the metal dishes decoration is obtained from the hammer blows when sinking.
Could the flutes from the carving chisel have been exploited in the wooden dish?

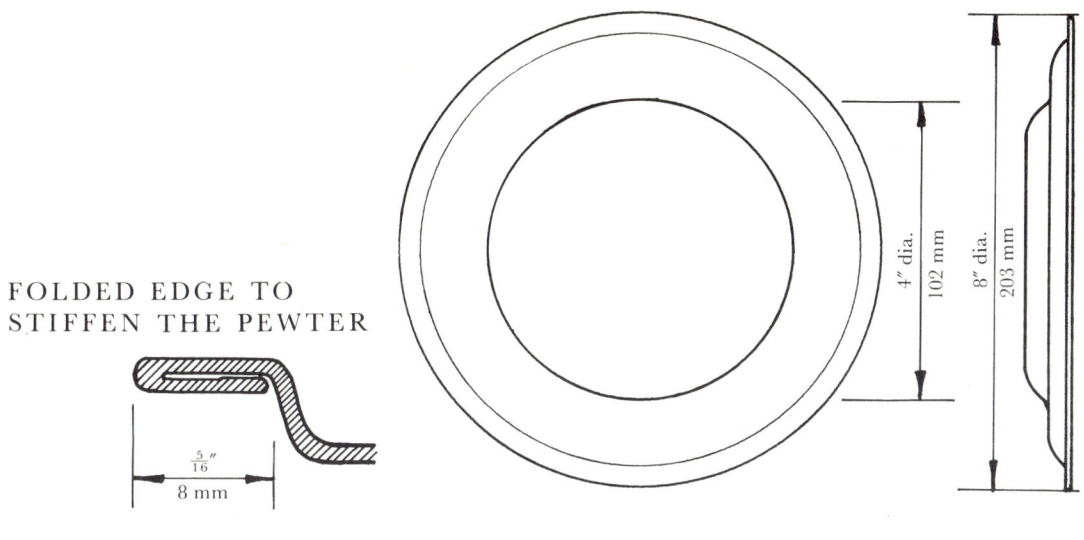

FOLDED EDGE TO
STIFFEN THE PEWTER

4″ dia.
102 mm

8″ dia.
203 mm

$\frac{5}{16}$″
8 mm

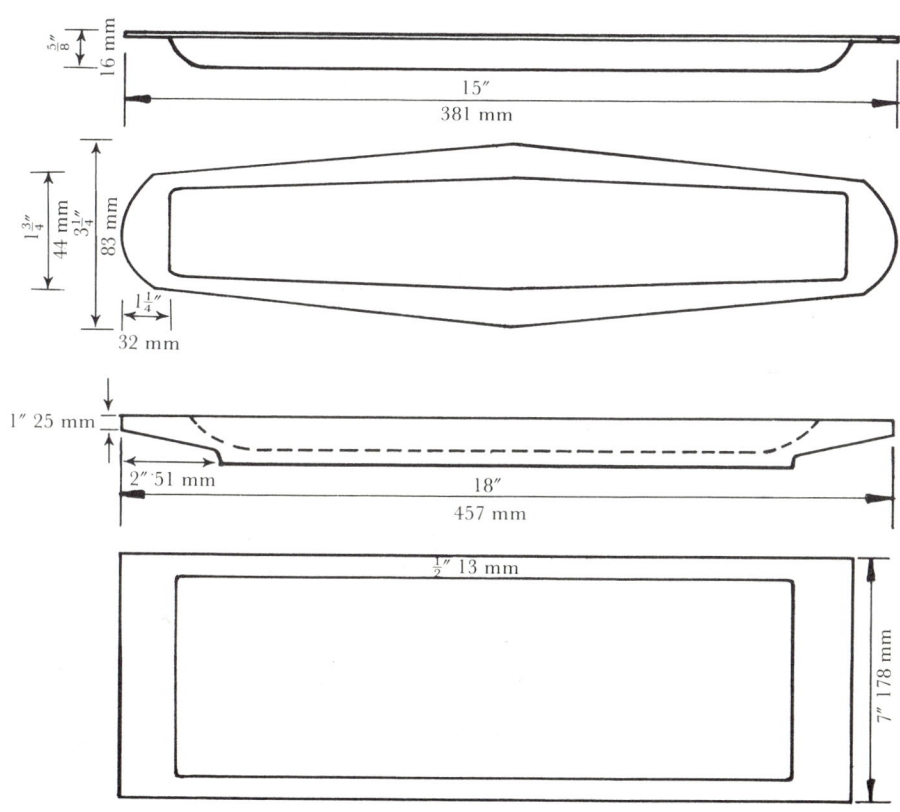

$\frac{5}{8}$
16 mm

15″
381 mm

$1\frac{3}{4}$″
44 mm
$3\frac{1}{4}$″
83 mm

$1\frac{1}{4}$″
32 mm

1″ 25 mm

2″ 51 mm

18″
457 mm

$\frac{1}{2}$″ 13 mm

7″ 178 mm

Ash tray and candle holder

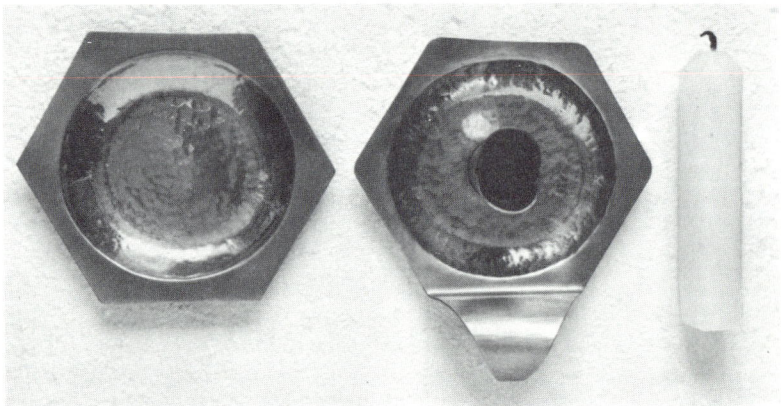

The hammered, polished, circular centres contrast with the smooth, matt, hexagonal surrounds.

The ferrule takes standard size candles and its flower-like split acts as a sharpener when a candle is twisted into place.

The simple handle flows naturally from the base.

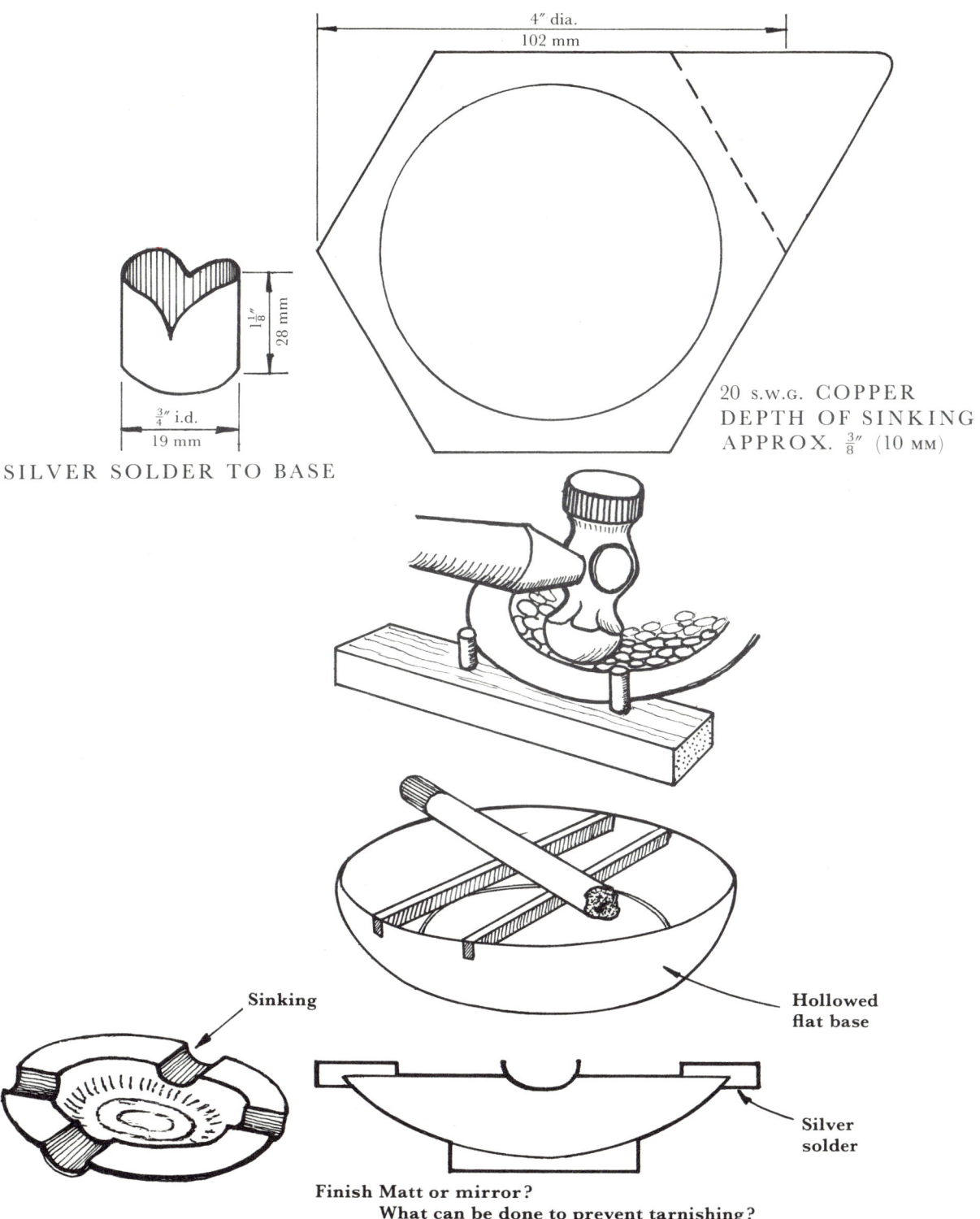

4″ dia.
102 mm

$1\frac{1}{8}$″
28 mm

$\frac{3}{4}$″ i.d.
19 mm

SILVER SOLDER TO BASE

20 s.w.g. COPPER
DEPTH OF SINKING
APPROX. $\frac{3}{8}$″ (10 ᴍᴍ)

Sinking

Hollowed
flat base

Silver
solder

Finish Matt or mirror?
What can be done to prevent tarnishing?

Ash tray and candle holder 101

Candlesticks

A casting of aluminium alloy with an anodised finish.

The holder and the candle, like the lamp and shade, form a composite whole. Stability is ensured by feeding the candle through from below. Could the construction be simplified by the use of a more malleable material?

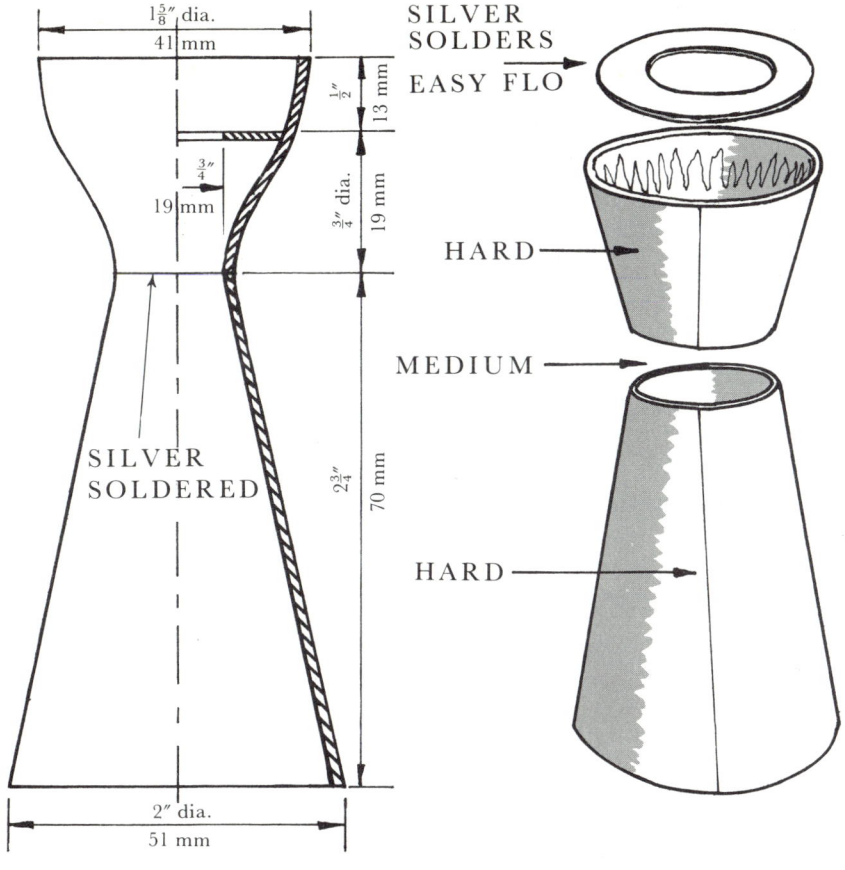

$1\frac{5}{8}''$ dia.

41 mm

$\frac{1}{2}''$ 13 mm

$\frac{3}{4}''$ 19 mm

$\frac{3}{4}''$ dia. 19 mm

SILVER
SOLDERED

$2\frac{3}{4}''$ 70 mm

2″ dia.

51 mm

SILVER
SOLDERS

EASY FLO

HARD

MEDIUM

HARD

After seaming the
top is contracted
and flared to shape
as on page 51

Casting possibilities

Aluminium
alloy-anodised finish

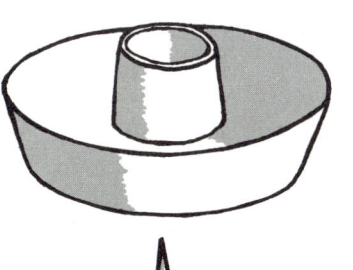

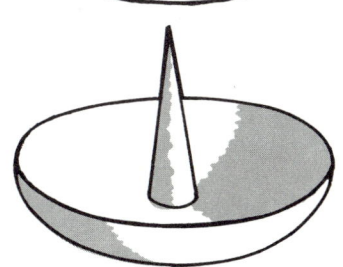

A deep bowl to catch wax.   Or non drip candles.

Must be stable, not easily knocked over

Spike, ferrule or hole to hold the candle?

Some beautiful examples of wrought iron candlesticks are shown
in the book 'Wrought Iron Work' by Fritz Kühn

Watering can

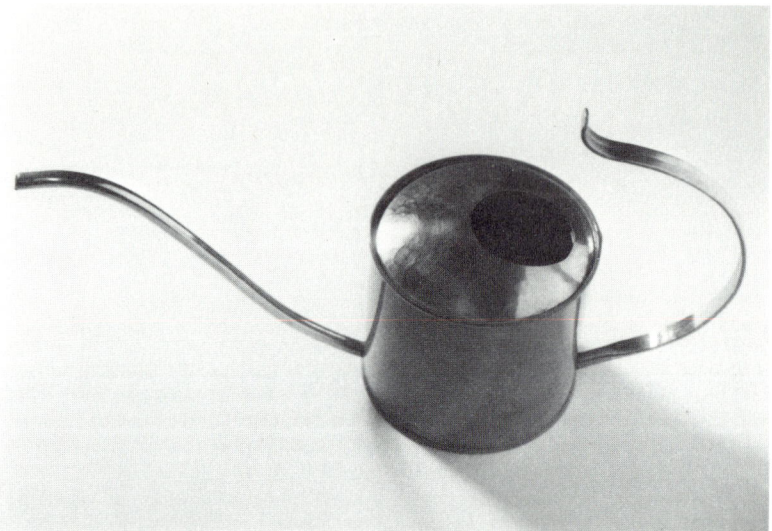

The separate curves formed by the handle and spout must complement each other. To simplify and strengthen the construction they are made from one piece of tubing, the handle area being flattened to make it easier to grip.

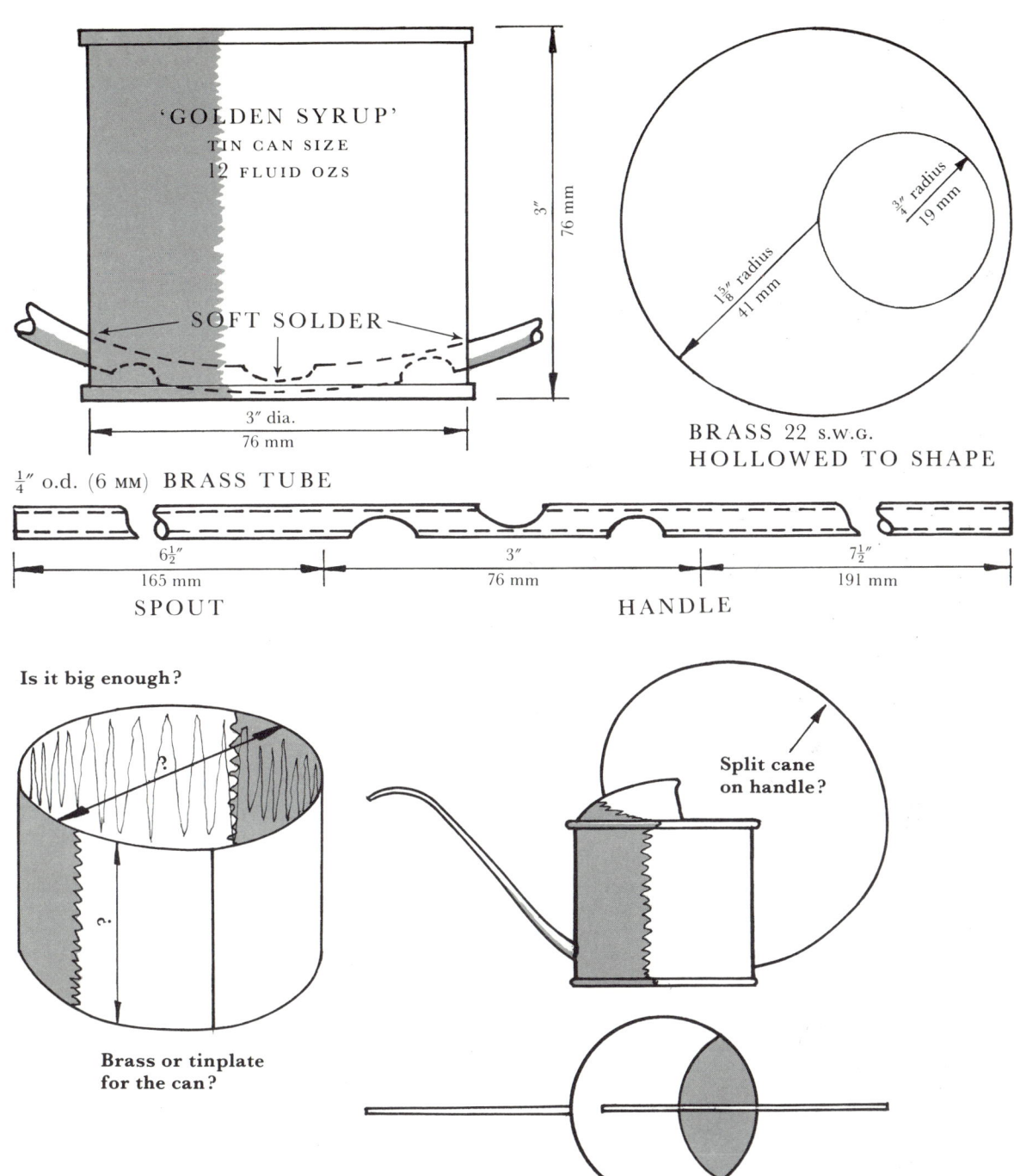

'GOLDEN SYRUP'
TIN CAN SIZE
12 FLUID OZS

3"
76 mm

SOFT SOLDER

3" dia.
76 mm

$1\frac{5}{8}$" radius
41 mm

$\frac{3}{4}$" radius
19 mm

BRASS 22 S.W.G.
HOLLOWED TO SHAPE

$\frac{1}{4}$" o.d. (6 MM) BRASS TUBE

$6\frac{1}{2}$"
165 mm

3"
76 mm

$7\frac{1}{2}$"
191 mm

SPOUT

HANDLE

Is it big enough?

?

?

Brass or tinplate
for the can?

Split cane
on handle?

Flower pot holder

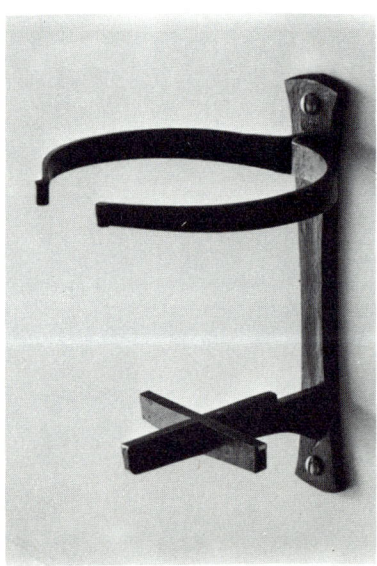

With forged work of this nature the texture of the iron can be emphasised by burnishing with a wire brush.

Brazing will discolour the metal and should be left to those instances where a painted finish is necessary, as in outdoor articles.

The top ring is not designed to grip the pots but to ensure that they will not be knocked off accidentally.

The brass dish holds flower pots of up to $3\frac{1}{2}''$ (89 mm) base diameter. This dish can be removed easily for cleaning yet is held securely by means of its set-in base.

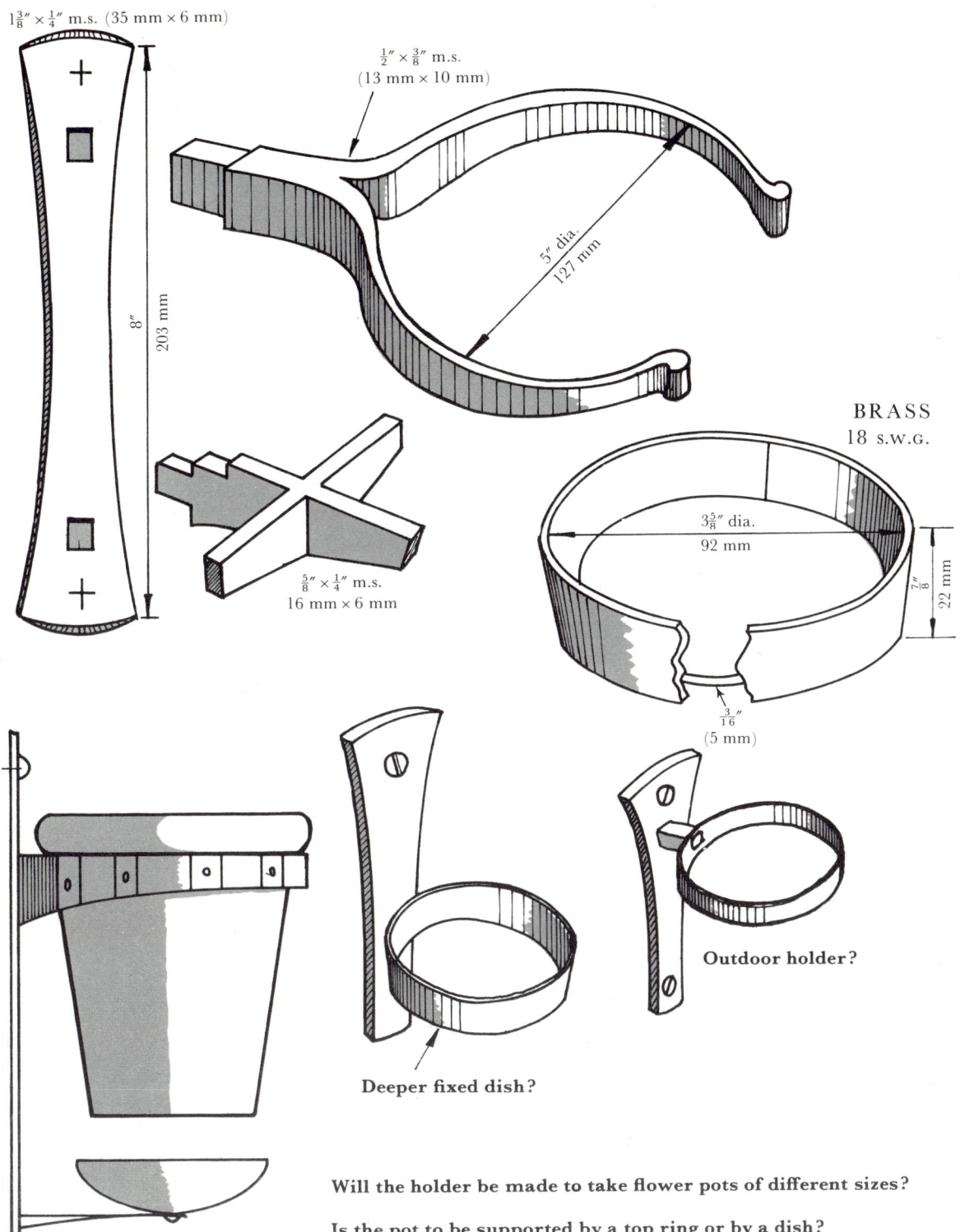

$1\frac{3}{8}'' \times \frac{1}{4}''$ m.s. (35 mm × 6 mm)

8″
203 mm

$\frac{1}{2}'' \times \frac{3}{8}''$ m.s.
(13 mm × 10 mm)

5″ dia.
127 mm

$\frac{5}{8}'' \times \frac{1}{4}''$ m.s.
16 mm × 6 mm

BRASS
18 s.w.g.

$3\frac{5}{8}''$ dia.
92 mm

$\frac{7}{8}''$
22 mm

$\frac{3}{16}''$
(5 mm)

Deeper fixed dish?

Outdoor holder?

Will the holder be made to take flower pots of different sizes?

Is the pot to be supported by a top ring or by a dish?

Fireside brush
and shovel

A rectangular brush can be obtained with some difficulty, but
follows the outline of the shovel more closely.

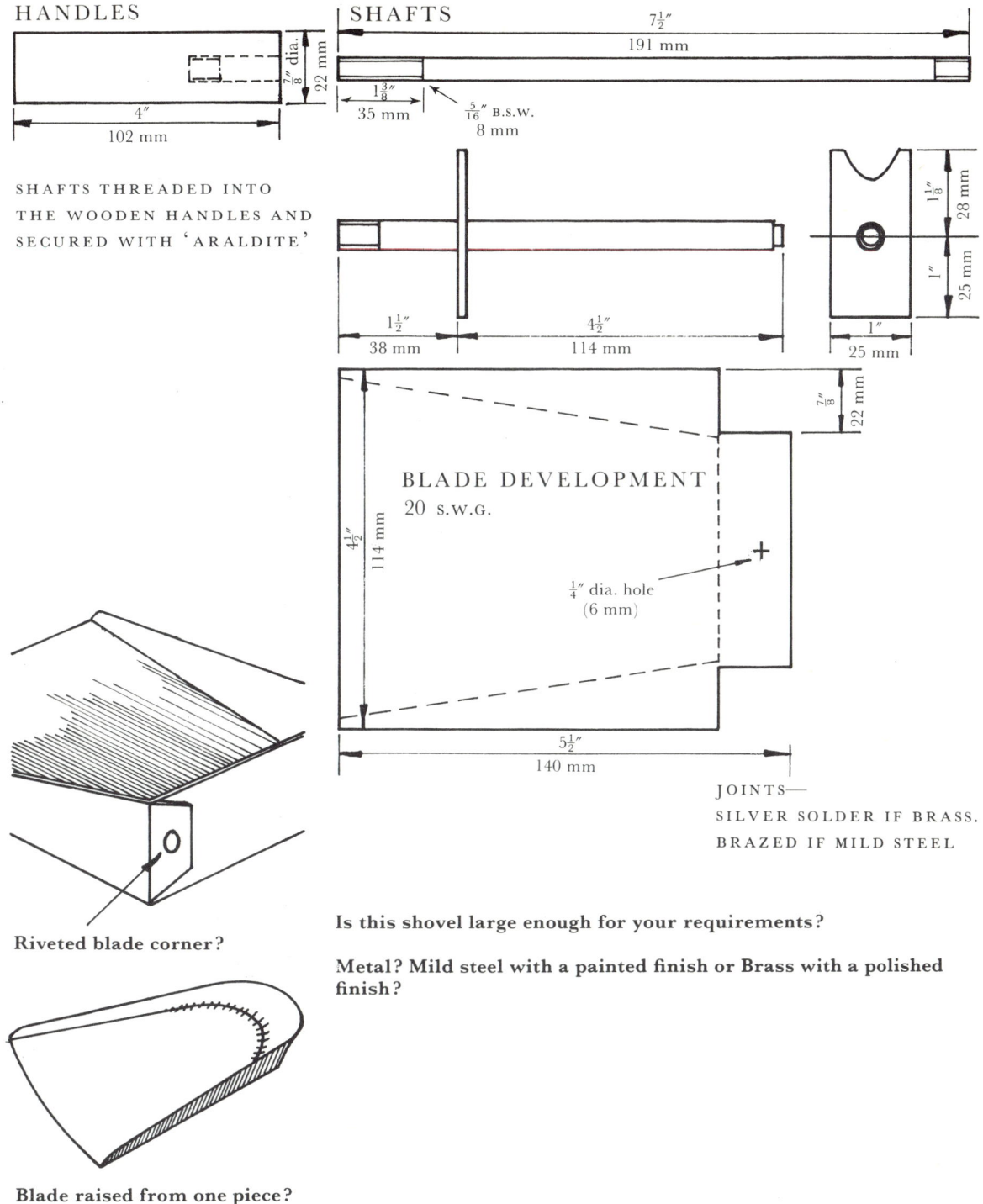

HANDLES

SHAFTS THREADED INTO
THE WOODEN HANDLES AND
SECURED WITH 'ARALDITE'

SHAFTS

BLADE DEVELOPMENT
20 S.W.G.

$\frac{1}{4}$″ dia. hole
(6 mm)

JOINTS—
SILVER SOLDER IF BRASS.
BRAZED IF MILD STEEL

Riveted blade corner?

Blade raised from one piece?

Is this shovel large enough for your requirements?

Metal? Mild steel with a painted finish or Brass with a polished finish?

Shoe horn

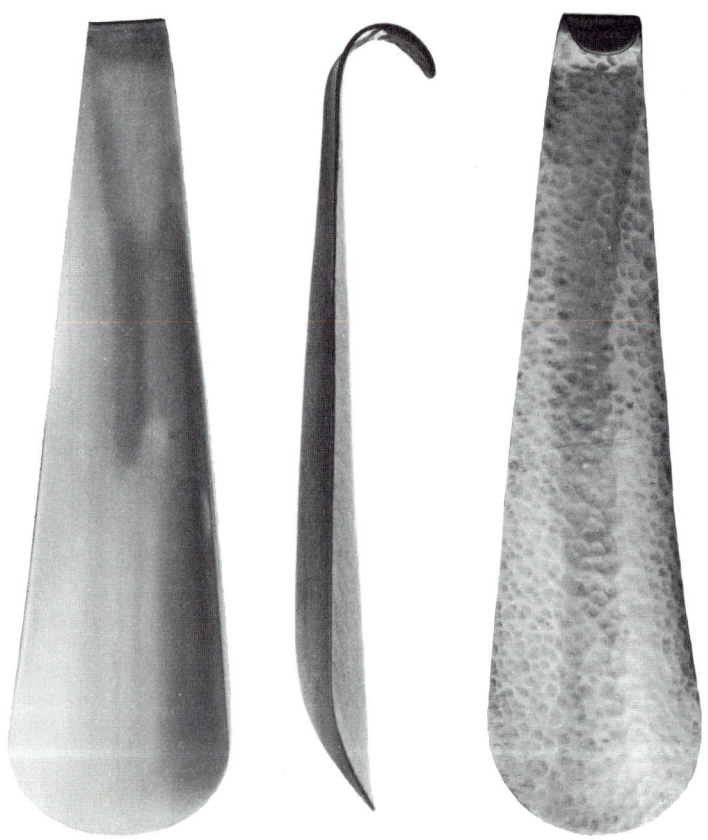

A simple functional shape, pleasing when viewed from any angle.

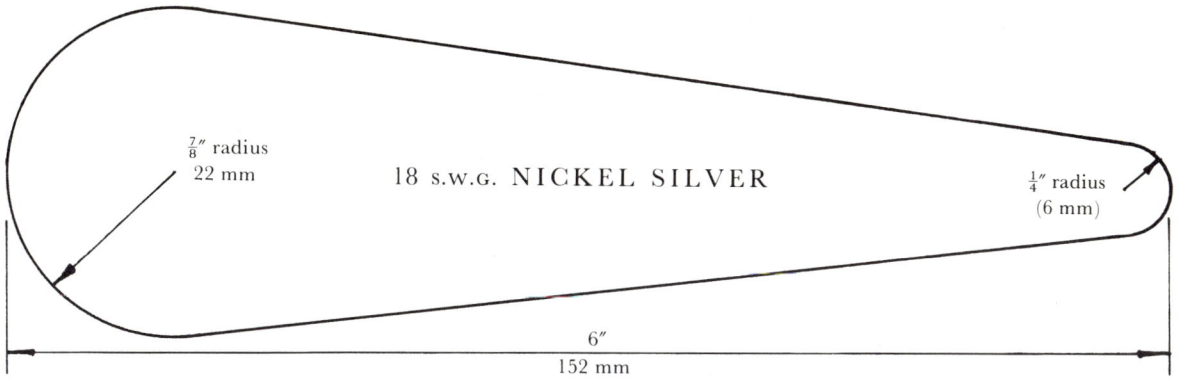

$\frac{7}{8}''$ radius
22 mm

18 s.w.g. NICKEL SILVER

$\frac{1}{4}''$ radius
(6 mm)

6"
152 mm

BACK OF SHOEHORN HAMMERED TO GIVE A CONTRASTING TEXTURE

Will this size fit your heel?

A tinplate or aluminium model before deciding on sizes and shape

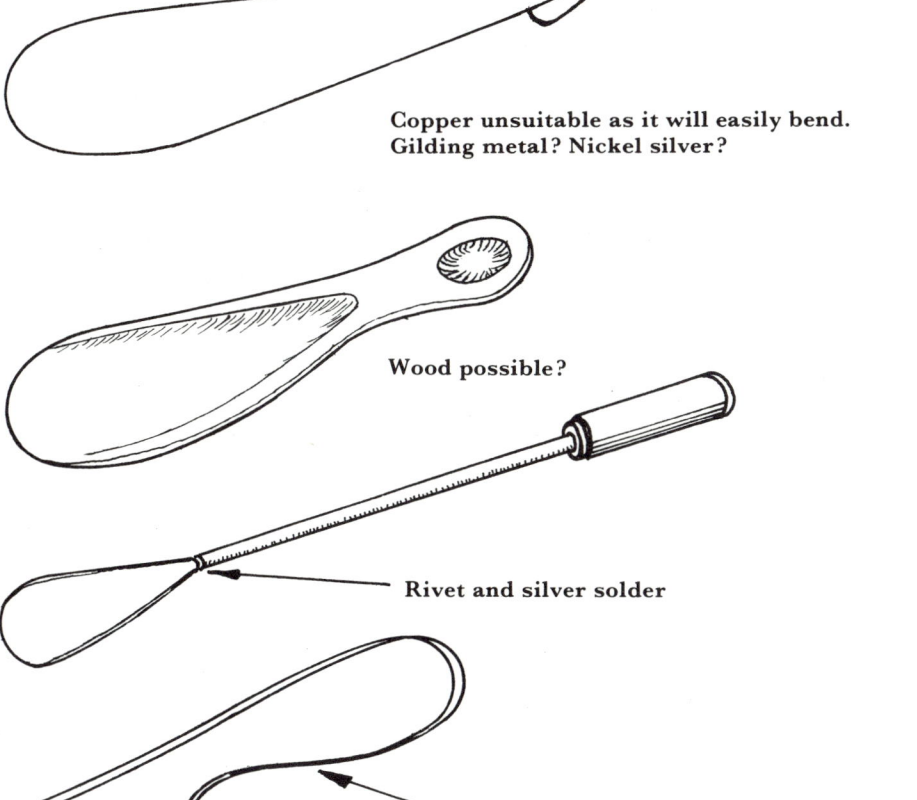

Hole useful?

Copper unsuitable as it will easily bend.
Gilding metal? Nickel silver?

Wood possible?

Rivet and silver solder

Shaft flattened and curved to form a handle

Boot scraper

The use of metal and concrete allows the scraper to be a simple, stable construction, the twisting of the metal allowing it to be made from one strip.

The draft on the sides of the concrete moulding box allows the box to be easily removed in one piece and so used again.

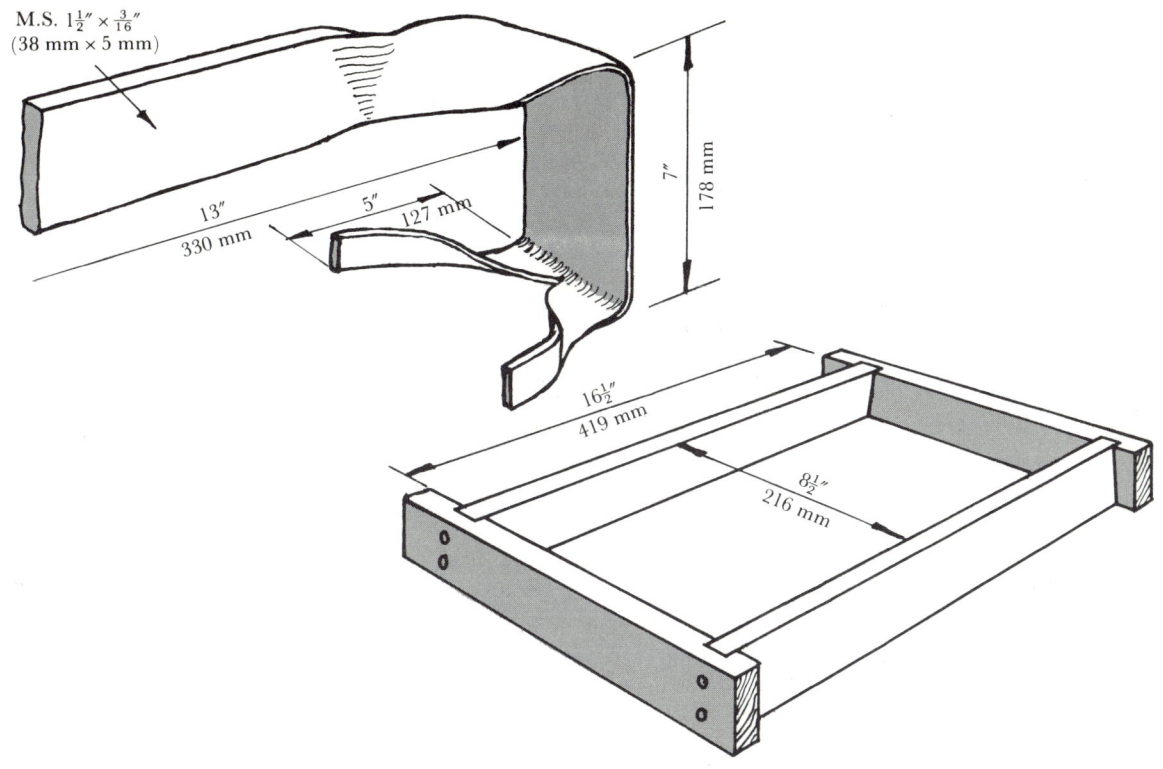

M.S. $1\frac{1}{2}'' \times \frac{3}{16}''$
(38 mm × 5 mm)

13"
330 mm

5" 127 mm

7"
178 mm

$16\frac{1}{2}''$
419 mm

$8\frac{1}{2}''$
216 mm

SHUTTERING $3\frac{1}{2}'' \times \frac{7}{8}''$ (89 MM × 22 MM) SOFTWOOD
$\frac{1}{2}''$ (13 MM) DRAFT ON SIDES. PLANED SMOOTH INSIDE

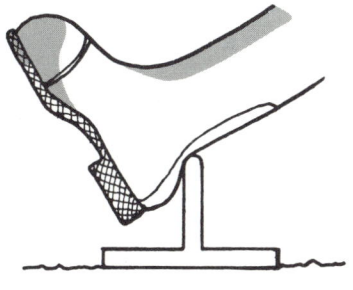

Will the scraper clean the boot's sole, side and toe cap?

Could the scraper also be used as a boot jack by tilting the bar?

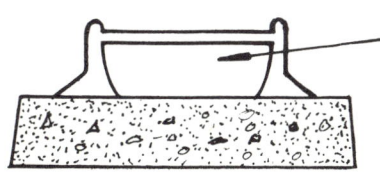

Make this wide enough to allow the boot underneath

Garden seats

An important constructional detail of these seats is the steel reinforcement in the concrete supports. The rods are threaded at the top where they protrude from the concrete, and so provide a secure fixing for the wooden seat. They also extend from the bottom where they are bent outwards to ensure a firm hold in the bedding concrete.

The tree seat is an extension of this idea. This particular seat was made by a group of 14-year-old boys.

MOULDING BOX

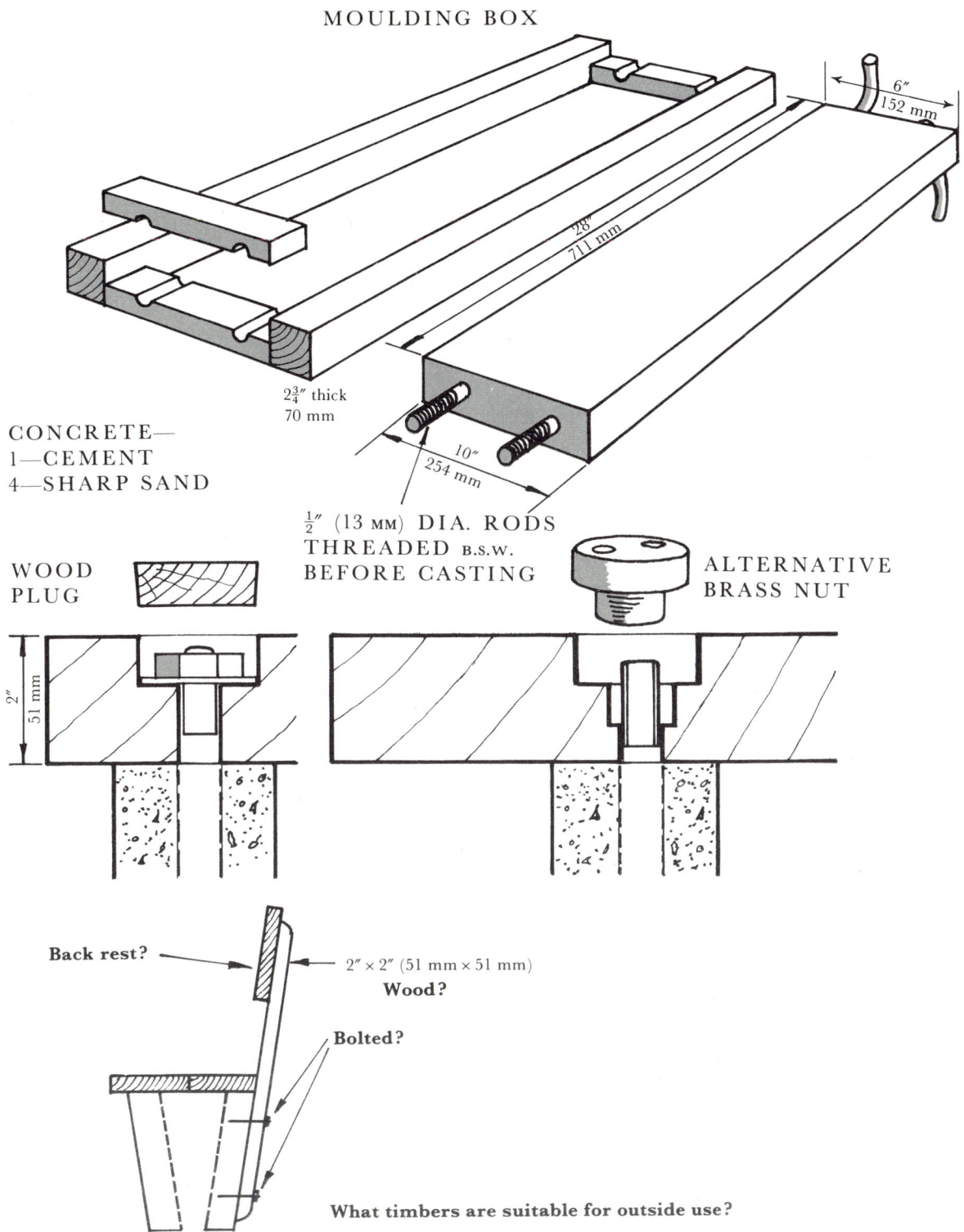

6″
152 mm

28″
711 mm

2¾″ thick
70 mm

CONCRETE—
1—CEMENT
4—SHARP SAND

10″
254 mm

½″ (13 ΜΜ) DIA. RODS
THREADED B.S.W.
BEFORE CASTING

WOOD
PLUG

2″
51 mm

ALTERNATIVE
BRASS NUT

Back rest? ← 2″ × 2″ (51 mm × 51 mm)
Wood?

Bolted?

What timbers are suitable for outside use?

Material	Supplier and address
Turnery discs	Fitchett & Woollacott Ltd., Popham Street, Nottingham
Lampshade materials, cane, etc.	Dryad Handicrafts, Northgate, Leicester
Lampshade materials, etc.	Arts & Crafts, 10 Byram Street, Huddersfield
String for chairs and stools	Healey Bros., Cartridge Street, Heywood, Lancashire
Polythene stoppers for salt pots	Griffin & George, Ealing Road, Alperton, Wembley, Middlesex
Tubing (square and round); welded (semi-bright finish)	Bayswater Tubes & Sections, Ltd., Foundry Works, Pencoed, Nr. Bridgend, Glamorgan
Mild steel (bright; free cutting quality)	Macready's Usaspead Corner, Pentonville Road, London N.1.
Copper, gilding metal (good return on scrap)	Enfield Rolling Mills Ltd., Brimsdown, Enfield, Middlesex
Stainless steel	Samuel Fox & Co. Ltd., Stocksbridge Works, Sheffield
Small quantities of non-ferrous metals	Clay Metal Supplies Ltd., 68 Springbridge Road, Ealing, London W.5
Sterling silver	Johnson Matthey & Co. Ltd., Hatton Garden, London E.C.1; also at Victoria Street, Birmingham 1 and 75 Eyre Street, Sheffield 1
Silver plating	Knights Silversmiths, Stanley Road, Wellingborough, Northants
Jewellery findings and pottery stones, thin sheet pewter and copper	Southern Handicrafts Ltd., 25 Kensington Gardens, Brighton
Jewellery enamels	W. G. Ball Ltd., Department J., Anchor Road, Longton, Stoke on Trent
Gem stones and jewellery findings	Messrs. Fisher, 43 Hazlewood Road, Northampton
Semi-precious stones	C. Lowe & Co. Ltd., 73 Spencer Street, Birmingham 18

Suggested further reading

Title	Author	Publisher
Creative Casting.	Choate	George Allen & Unwin
Looking and Seeing—Bks. 1–4.	Kurt Rowland	Ginn
The Nature of Design.	David Pye	Studio Vista
Designs in Metal.	Paul Bridge and Austin Crossland	Batsford
Contemporary Design in Metalwork.	Brian Larkman with S. H. Glenister	John Murray
Contemporary Design in Woodwork—Vols. 1 and 2.	S. H. Glenister	John Murray
Decorative Art Year Book.		Studio Vista
Looking at Furniture.	Sir Gordon Russell	Lund Humphries
British Furniture Today.	Erno Goldfinger	Alex Tiranti
Foundation of Design in Wood.	Francis O. Zanker	Dryad Press
Handmade Woodwork of the Twentieth Century.	A. E. Bradshaw	John Murray
Creative Woodcraft.	Ernst Rottger	Batsford
Sculpture in Wood.	Edward Norman	Alex Tiranti
An Approach to Design in Metal.	Vincent Austin	Macmillan
The Design and Creation of Jewelry.	Robert Von Newmann	Pitman
Designing and Making Handwrought Jewelry.	Joseph F. Schoenfelt	McGraw-Hill
Form in Nature and Life.	Andreas Feininger	Thames & Hudson
Design Centre Publications.		
Decorative Work in Wrought Iron.	Fritz Kühn	Harrap
Metalwork and Its Decoration by Etching.	O. Almedia	Mills & Boon
The Technique of Enamelling.	Geoffrey Clarke, Francis and Ida Feher	Batsford
Jewelry Making for the Amateur.	Klares Lewes	Batsford
Woodturning Design and Practice.	G. T. James	John Murray
The Practical Wood Turner.	F. Pain	Evans Bros.

Metric conversion table

The metric measurements on our working drawings and on this page have been converted to the nearest whole millimetre. A slide for converting non-metric to metric measurements can be obtained from British Standards Institution, 101/113 Pentonville Road, London, N.1.

	ENGLISH	METRIC
Parts of inch to the nearest whole millimetre	$\frac{1}{16}''$	2 mm
	$\frac{1}{8}''$	3 mm
	$\frac{3}{16}''$	5 mm
	$\frac{1}{4}''$	6 mm
	$\frac{5}{16}''$	8 mm
	$\frac{3}{8}''$	10 mm
	$\frac{7}{16}''$	11 mm
	$\frac{1}{2}''$	13 mm
	$\frac{9}{16}''$	14 mm
	$\frac{5}{8}''$	16 mm
	$\frac{11}{16}''$	17 mm
	$\frac{3}{4}''$	19 mm
	$\frac{13}{16}''$	21 mm
	$\frac{7}{8}''$	22 mm
	$\frac{15}{16}''$	24 mm
Inches to the nearest whole millimetre	1″	25 mm
	2″	51 mm
	3″	76 mm
	4″	102 mm
	5″	127 mm
	6″	152 mm
	7″	178 mm
	8″	203 mm
	9″	229 mm
	10″	254 mm
	11″	279 mm
Feet to the nearest whole millimetre	1′	305 mm
	2′	610 mm
	3′	914 mm
	4′	1220 mm
	5′	1520 mm